Commendations for ]

# WEARING

*Exploring the Biblical In*

'I was immediately intrigued when Frances mentioned the idea of writing a book about what we wear and our relationship with clothing, both literally and symbolically. The result of her labours is a refreshing, mind opening and challenging book which made me look at myself and the things of God in a different light. I enjoyed reading it for my personal study but think, with its thought provoking questions at the end of each chapter, that it would make an excellent book for group discussion.'

—Canon Judy Hirst, *Diocesan Missioner, Durham Diocese, Spiritual Director and Retreat Leader*

'*Wearing Well* provokes us to think deeply about an everyday subject: our clothes. Each chapter guides us through a wealth of biblical material and concludes with some penetrating questions. Thoughtful yet highly accessible, this is an excellent book for small group study and discussion.'

—The Rt. Revd. Dr. Robert Innes, *Bishop of the Church of England Diocese in Europe*

# WEARING WELL

*Exploring the Biblical Imagery of Clothing*

Frances Shaw

Regent College Publishing
www.regentpublishing.com

Published 2019 by Regent College Publishing
5800 University Boulevard, Vancouver, BC V6T 2E4 Canada

Regent College Publishing is an imprint of the Regent Bookstore
<www.regentbookstore.com>. Views expressed in works pub-
lished by Regent College Publishing are those of the author and
do not necessarily represent the official position of Regent College
<www.regent-college.edu>.

ISBN 978-1-57383-576-3

Cataloguing-in-Publication Data is on file at Library and Archives
Canada

# Contents

# Foreword

I've been fascinated by Paul's image of 'putting on the Lord Jesus Christ' ever since I saw a preacher pull on a surplice over his other clothing and stand before us in the pulpit covered in Christ (Rom. 13:14).

I might have been even more engaged had I been there when the 19th century preacher Billy Bray took off most of his clothes in the pulpit to illustrate the need to strip off the old self (Col. 3:9). I'd love to know if he was asked back.

These are powerful images. Clearly there's something important going on in the way we choose to present ourselves. But how much do we explore the way we dress, and interrogate our choices, in the light of our faith?

Frances Shaw has done a fascinating job of asking pertinent questions about what we choose to wear in this fashion-saturated culture, and views them through a clear biblical lens. She sets up the contemporary questions and then takes us on an exhilarating journey through the Bible and pulls out material many of us will never have thought about in these terms.

Change of status is often reflected in changes in what people wear; is it different when someone takes on a new identity in Christ, and if so, how and why? How do our actions reflect the fact that we have been clothed in Christ? Have we explored what being naked before God really means? Is there an expected dress code in our own church? Is it Christian to say 'I don't care what I wear'? How do looks matter for a Christian? And then, fascinatingly, have we noticed all the references to clothing in the passion narratives?

This is rich material, and Frances ends each chapter with strangely penetrating questions. After I read this book I was left with many stimulating questions running around my head. But one in particular: why has this kind of creative exploration not been done before?

Well, it has now. Enjoy.

+John Pritchard, *Bishop of Oxford, 2007–2014*

# Acknowledgements

I feel a certain sense of irony and perhaps mystery that I come to be writing about clothing. I seem to be cold most of the time and spend about six months of the year wearing a woolly hat, along with what could be described as smart-casual, verging on casual clothes. I positively dislike shopping for clothes and have a few favourites which come out all the time. So why am I writing about the biblical language and imagery to do with clothing?

In reading Scripture, I was challenged by Paul's phrase, 'put on the Lord Jesus Christ' (Rom. 13:14). What exactly might that mean? And how can you put on a person? Is it more than 'putting on' certain qualities or virtues? A commentary told me that there is little evidence that this metaphor of 'putting on a person' was widely used, and may in fact have been unique to Paul. It finds some parallels in drama, where an actor may be said to 'put on' the part of the person they are acting. But surely in faith terms there is more than acting involved here.

This then led me to think further about other language connected with clothing. I was intrigued, and that started a more extended exploration, not only of 'putting on' and other metaphors to do with clothing, but also the whole concept of clothing—the quality of it, or the lack of it, and what it symbolises, both in terms of our society in general, and in religious terms. Over several years, I have also found myself alert to other clothing references and metaphors, from white wedding dresses to black funeral wear or the symbolic use of red by King Henry VIII, but not by Queen Elizabeth I.

My husband, Peter, frequently lectures at the summer school at Regent College, Vancouver. I am very grateful to him for his encouragement, and that these visits have enabled me to make use of their excellent library, as well as to meet up with Bill Reimer their Bookstore and Publications Manager. Thanks are also due to Bill for his support, along with Robert Hand and Caroline Ahn in taking this work to publication.

Thanks are also due to Stephen Barton for sending emails detailing books and articles referencing clothing as and when he came across them. I also sincerely appreciate the support and encouragement of long-standing friends and colleagues, especially John Pritchard, Judy Hirst and Robert Innes for their kind words about the text included here.

This project has been some years in coming to fruition. My children have been enthusiastic of my endeavours: Colin for bringing his analytical and managerial background; Graham for taking the themes through into a Lent and Easter sermon series; and Ruth for swapping interesting ideas and occasionally swapping clothes. Wider family and local church members have helped me to pursue, and hopefully embody, what it might mean to be 'clothed with Christ'.

# Introduction

We live near the entrance to a sixth form college and over 2,000 students come and go every day. Every year they used to organise a rag week, and those not wearing the designated clothes for the day had to pay a fine for charity. There was a regular old school uniform day, pyjama day, Hawaiian day and so on. When our children were young, they used to watch these apparitions going past our house.

'Mummy, why are they wearing those funny clothes'?

'Well, each day this week they are dressing up to raise money for charity. I think today it might be pyjamas. Let's see what it is tomorrow'.

Some weeks later, gazing out of the window:

'Mummy, what day is it today'?

'Tuesday'.

'No, I mean what dressing up day is it today'?

'Oh, I don't think they're dressing up today; the week's finished. That's just what they normally wear'.

Our language is full of references to clothing, in sayings and metaphors: blanket condemnation; duvet days; belt and braces; pull your socks up; apron strings; cloak and dagger; bib and tucker; shoe horn; kid gloves; mad hatter;

well dressing.[1]

So what is clothing for? Like all mammals, we are born without clothing, but instead of growing fur or a thick skin, we are wrapped up, and spend the rest of our lives in various forms of clothes. Clothing can be useful, for protection and modesty. Clothing can be creative, to express ourselves in various colours and styles. Clothing can reflect our status, in the broadest sense of that word; and clothing is a social tool, conveying individual or group identity. Clothing is a 'language' symbolically expressing style, status, values and aspirations.

Clothes are not only literally 'all over us' but they are also all around us. What you wear and when you wear it, can be difficult to negotiate. 'Just come as you are' is not always very helpful. We prefer some kind of indicator as to what is acceptable, and what everyone else will be wearing. A garden party has completely different connotations to 'we'll just be in the garden'; suits and hats appropriate for one and shorts and sandals for the other.

To resolve this dilemma, invitations often indicate what is to be worn: from 'medals, but not swords', to black tie, to formal, to lounge suits, to smart casual, to casual. Our youngest son turned up at his Duke of Edinburgh's gold award presentation at St. James' Palace wearing a sky blue suit with a pink lining, and was deemed to be an art student (which he wasn't). His logic was that the invitation said, 'suits' to be worn, but did not specify 'dark suits', or 'formal suits'. He had the confidence to carry it off, and enjoyed himself.

So, does what you see on the outside reflect what's going on in the inside? The type of clothes you wear can be a symbolic representation of your status—both inwardly and outwardly. They say something about who you are—or who you think you are—or who you want others to think you are—or who you would like to be. This is a complex area, both in terms of what is socially acceptable, as well as comfortable for the individual. The element of anxiety over making the correct choice, can result in flinging open the wardrobe door and declaring, 'I've got nothing to wear'!

Clothes have a certain power and influence. If the Duchess of Cambridge is seen wearing something from a high street brand, the item is sold out within hours—a similar effect to a well known chef recommending a certain frying pan or the use of cranberries. The fashion industry is hugely creative and innovative, developing new kinds of fabrics, colours and styles. But it can also play on our insecurities in a somewhat superficial way. The word 'fashion' can be a verb—to mould or to shape, as in clay to a pot. 'Fashion' can also be used as a noun, 'It is the fashion'—meaning trend or influence, usually referring to clothing. We can see how, in some sense, fashion meaning apparel, also fashions us, precisely because of the way in which clothing shapes us.

We often develop an attachment to our favourite clothes. One day you notice your 'new' sweatshirt isn't looking quite so new—no longer smart casual, merely casual. You still wear it, love it, but over time it gets further downgraded until eventually it ends up in the pile on the floor to wear in the garden. You still feel comfortable in it and love it, but finally when it's covered in holes and bits of paint, it has to go out. Having to say goodbye can feel a bit like a bereavement. You really miss your old friend.

The Dutch Christian, Corrie ten Boom, in Ravensbruck

concentration camp during the Second World War, after her sister, Betsie, had died, found her blue sweater on top of a pile of clothes heaped in the hallway.

> I stooped to pick it up. The sweater was threadbare and stained with newsprint, but it was a tangible link with Betsie. Mien seized my arm. "Don't touch those things! Black lice! They'll all be burned."
>
> And so I left behind the last physical tie. It was just as well. It was better. Now what tied me to Betsie was the hope of heaven.[2]

In Scripture, this transient or temporary nature of clothes, and the fact that they wear out, is recognised and contrasted with God's eternal love:

> Long ago you laid the foundation of the earth,
>   And the heavens are the work of your hands.
> They will perish, but you endure;
>   They will all wear out like a garment.
> You change them like clothing, and they pass away;
>   But you are the same, and your years have no end.
>                           Ps. 102:25–27; Heb. 1:10, 11

Using similar language, Jesus teaches his disciples,

> Do not store up for yourselves treasures on earth, where moth and rust consume and where thieves break in and steal; but store up for yourselves treasures in heaven where neither moth nor rust consumes and where thieves do not break in and steal.
>
>                           Matt. 6:19, 20

In the book of Samuel, we read that Hannah provided a little robe each year for her son Samuel, whom she had dedicated to serve the Lord in the temple at Shiloh (1 Sam. 2:18, 19). While Hannah's provision is seen as part of her devotion to God and thanksgiving for the gift of Samuel, from a mother's perspective, I can imagine her weaving such a garment in tears as a reminder of the painful separation from her son.

Samuel's robe also has a symbolic meaning. We read that 'Samuel was ministering before the Lord, a boy wearing a linen ephod' (1 Sam. 2:18). This indicates that Samuel is already a priest, a mini-priest, because an ephod is a priestly garment, plain linen for priests, embroidered and coloured for the High Priest (1 Sam. 2:28; Ex. 28:4). There may also be an intended contrast here with current priest, Eli, and his two sons, who should have been good and holy priests, but were not.

These various examples show how clothing, in a physical and tangible way, is a significant part of our everyday lives. Language about clothing also functions in a metaphorical or symbolic way. These two aspects, physical and symbolic, overlap in many different ways. The following chapters set out to explore some of these aspects as well as how we might think about the impact language and imagery about clothing may have on the way we live our lives now.

Some of the different examples and references may seem to jump about a bit. This is partly deliberate in order to show how varied and multifaceted the language and ideas related to clothing can be. Some of the examples given could fit well in different chapters—'fit well', another use of clothing language.

Samuel's ephod indicated that he was a priest, and many forms of clothing will show what kind of status you have. In our culture that can be status in social terms (class), what kind of work you do (or not), what kind of authority you have, and to which group you belong. So changing your clothes can indicate, amongst other things, a change in your status, and this will be explored in the next chapter.

In religious terms, we have a status in relation to God. Those who have 'put on Christ' need also to put on, as well as practise, certain virtues as befits this status. The moral implications of this changed status will be explored in chapter 3.

If you are naked, that too tells you something about your status, that is, probably poor and vulnerable. But spiritually, there is a sense in which we are all naked before God. He knows us and who we are in our bodies, with no coverings to hide under. This sense of nakedness and our relationship with our bodies is explored in chapter 4.

Our relationship with God is not solely an individual one. We are also members of his people, his church, and we become related to those who have also changed their status. Clothing becomes an indication of the group to which we belong. The status of kinship as a member of a group can be in either a voluntary sense or a forced sense, and instances of both co-operation and deviance are covered in chapter 5.

Not all church cultures are the same: in some it really doesn't matter what you wear; in others clothing plays a much more significant part. Should Christians have any different kind of attitude to clothes and what they wear? Or is this not really very important? And is it possible to tell a group of Christians by what they are wearing? These questions are explored in chapter 6.

There are many references to clothing throughout the passion narratives, and these will be covered in chapter 7, before drawing some of these threads together at the end.

In Acts 9:36 we read about Tabitha/Dorcas, the only woman in the NT described as a 'disciple', 'devoted to good works and acts of charity', making tunics and other clothing. She, along with Lydia from Thyatira, a 'dealer in purple cloth' (Acts 16:14), were believers in God and followers of Jesus. This book seeks to explore our relationship with clothing, both literally and symbolically in some every day as well as Christian ways. This is not straightforward, but I hope that it will generate some new ways of looking at the subject as well as stimulating discussion—of something that is literally all around us.

## Discussion

1.  Think about your relationship with your clothes.
2.  As an exercise: think about all you are wearing today and any stories connected with each item—where you bought it, how much it cost, who you were with at the time, when you last wore it, etc.
3.  Do you feel that what you choose to wear expresses your own creativity, or a conformity to some other expectations or standards? Or maybe a bit of both.

# 1

## WHERE DID YOU GET THAT HAT?
### *Indications of Status*

Status is a strange thing, and the kind of clothes that go with it can be hard to figure out. Generally the kind of clothes we choose to wear says something our socio-economic status—who we are socially, economically or in terms of our role or profession. Our clothes may also say something more general in terms of our emotional state, and they also have an important symbolic role in identifying people, and at times of transition from one state to another.

Those who are well off financially tend to wear better clothes, while those who are poor do not. The trouble today is that you can't always tell someone's status by what they are wearing. There are those who dress up, because they aspire to a different social status. There are those of a 'higher' status, who deliberately dress down—the lord of the manor going round in old trousers and a patched jacket, type of thing.

Clothing can also often indicate what type of role you are performing, as in specific uniforms. A person in a suit probably works in an office; someone in overalls and boots may work on a building site. But of course such categories can be very fluid, as 'Dress Down Fridays' and very casual wear in some companies indicate. There are those who wear jeans to work, but who are also the owner or CEO of the company, as I discovered once when chatting to a plumber. There are those who genuinely want to or need to 'look the part'. There are those who pretend to be someone else, or represent something they are not. The variations are widespread and quite confusing.

Both the style and colour of your clothes can say a lot about your status. King Henry VIII was frequently shown in portraits wearing red velvet, not just because he thought it made him look more attractive, but to assert authority and power over his people. Red dye was very expensive, and velvet very costly. Henry also established a strict code where no one under the rank of Knight of the Garter was allowed to wear red velvet in their gowns.

The colour red also had far more negative connotations, especially when worn by a woman. She could be labelled a 'scarlet woman'[1] or called the 'Whore of Babylon' who is described as 'clothed in purple and scarlet, and adorned with gold and jewels and pearls, holding in her hand a golden cup full of abominations and the impurities of her fornication' (Rev. 17:4). As a female monarch aware of the symbolism attached both to her person and the colour red, Elizabeth I chose richly embroidered white satin gowns to demonstrate her wealth and power.[2]

When the Scottish poet, Robert Burns of *Auld Lang Syne* fame, finally married Jean Armour in 1788, the bride wore black, not as a sign of mourning, but as a status symbol. Black was one of the most expensive colours for cloth then available. Burns acquired it especially for her, and 15 yards of material arrived at the Ayrshire farmstead, coming all the way from Glasgow.

In Victorian society clothes were a very important marker of status. Poor women who only had one or two dresses, would dye a dress black to be seen as appropriately dressed for a period of mourning, and then later take this colour out of it. In a similar way, at a wedding for those with little money, the bride did not always wear white, but a dress of a different colour, which could then later be worn as 'best'. All this reflected the fact that you didn't want to be seen to be poor.

Clothing can also say something about what kind of 'state' you are in, whether you are on holiday or at work, happy or sad. Wearing black often shows that you are in a state of mourning. Queen Victoria wore black for 40 years, after the death of her beloved Albert at the age of 42 in 1861. Today, wearing mourning black is often limited to the day of the funeral, and sometimes not even that.

A deliberate change of clothing can symbolically indicate and express a change in status. In Roman society, boys aged 15 or 16 underwent a ceremony to mark puberty. Part of this involved changing from a child's clothing (*toga praetexta*) to adult dress (*toga virilis*). There does not appear to have been a similar ceremony for girls, as girls passed to womanhood at marriage. In a similar sort of way, getting to the 'status' of the school sixth form in the past could be demonstrated by a change from black to brown shoes; or the wearing of a suit instead of school uniform, with or without a coloured shirt; or perhaps no school uniform at all as a distinguishing mark.

What we wear often gives an indication of our status. The winner of the Masters Golf Tournament in Augusta wears a green jacket, and the winner of the Tour de France wears a yellow jersey. Those who achieve a place in the team also wear a team strip. Clothes can represent something we have achieved, or something we are. They can represent something we aspire to be. So clothes bearing the Nike swoosh tend to be worn by those who are in fact very fit. They are also worn by those who are definitely not fit, where what that brand represents becomes an aspiration. Clothes can also be used to cover up many imperfections or insecurities, and can represent something or someone we are not.

Many of these aspects of status—socio-economic, emotional state, as a way of identifying people, as well as transition from one status to another—are found in Bible.

In his letter, James poses the question to believers: 'Do you with your acts of favouritism really believe in our glorious Lord Jesus Christ'? As an example he describes how those who come to their assembly 'with gold rings and in fine clothes', are offered a seat; while a poor person who comes in 'dirty clothes' is told to 'Stand there' (Jas. 2:1–3).

The phrase 'sackcloth and ashes', indicates a state of mourning or repentance or remorse. For example, when Elijah convicted King Ahab about his deceitful acquisition of Naboth's vineyard,

> He tore his clothes and put sackcloth over his bare flesh; he fasted, lay in the sackcloth, and went about dejectedly.
>
> 1 Kings 21:27[3]

The stories about Elijah and Elisha in 1 and 2 Kings are also about status and role, how that is recognised, and how it is passed on from one to the other. The injured King Ahaziah had sent messengers to enquire of a foreign god as to whether he would recover. The messengers returned with a word from Elijah, who had met them on the way, and who said that the king was going to die.

> He said to them, 'What sort of man was he who came to meet you and told you these things'? They answered him, 'A hairy man, with a leather belt around his waist'. He said, 'It is Elijah the Tishbite'.
>
> 2 Kings 1:7, 8

So distinctive was Elijah's clothing, that even the King of Samaria knew who he was.

For those familiar with this story, the description of John the Baptist in the gospels would immediately resonate:

> Now John wore clothing of camel's hair with a leather belt around his waist, and his food was locusts and wild honey.
>
> Matt. 3:4

The garment and the belt are obviously significant, otherwise they wouldn't be mentioned. The clothing immediately links John with Elijah. 2 Kings 2:11 records that Elijah did not die but 'ascended in a whirlwind into heaven'. The assertion that he had not died, led to an expectation of his return, mentioned at the very end of the Old Testament:[4]

> 'Lo, I will send you the prophet Elijah before the great and terrible day of the Lord comes'.
>
> Mal. 4:5

So when John turns up in this distinctive clothing, this not only links him with Elijah himself, but also with the whole background and expectation of God's renewed activity. John is Jesus' forerunner, the messenger sent ahead, and he is known as such by the clothes he is wearing.

There are many and various parallels between John the Baptist and Jesus, whose lives are intimately connected. They both have unusual and miraculous births; they say similar things (repent); are understood by the people to be prophets; they create opposition and are rejected and executed as criminals.[5]

There are also various points at which there are significant differences between John and Jesus. Jesus did not baptise and John did not do miracles. While John's clothing was significant, in the gospels, there is no indication that Jesus' status was linked to his clothing, nor did people recognise who he was by what he was wearing.[6]

There are only a very few references to Jesus' clothes, such as his outer garment and tunic, both of which will be covered in more detail in chapter 7 when we come to look at the passion narratives. There is one reference to Jesus' cloak. Mark (5:27) records that a woman with severe bleeding came up behind Jesus in the crowd and 'touched his cloak, for she said, "If I but touch his clothes, I will be made well."' Matthew (9:21) says that she 'touched the fringe of his cloak'. The word for 'fringe' can refer to the edge or hem of the cloak, or to the blue and white tassels worn on the four corners of the outer cloak.[7] There is nothing particularly unusual or special about this attire for a male Jew of the time.

This particular story emphasises that it is the woman's faith that has saved/healed her and not just the touch. Yet Mark, in one of his summary passages, also records that crowds wanted to 'touch even the fringe of his cloak; and all who touched it were healed' (Mark 6:56; cf. 3:10). The transmission of divine power from a healer to clothing or cloth was well known at the time (see the reference to Paul's handkerchiefs or aprons in Acts 19:12).[8]

Apart from the garment and the belt, there is another particular piece of clothing associated with Elijah, and that is his 'mantle'. The word used here is a different one from the more usual one for 'cloak'.[9] Elijah had 'wrapped his face in his mantle' during his encounter with God on the mountain at Horeb. It was this mantle that he then threw over Elisha while he was ploughing to anoint him as a prophet (1 Kings 19:13, 16, 19). Later in the narrative the mantle is left behind for Elisha to pick up after Elijah's departure. This episode is concerned with the legitimate transfer of Elijah's prophetic powers and role to his successor, confirmed by enabling Elisha to do what Elijah had just done—parting the river Jordan by striking the water with the mantle (2 Kings 2:8, 13, 14).[10] We do not learn what happened to this mantle when Elisha died (2 Kings 13:20).

Today we use the expression ' taking on' or 'taking over' the mantle of someone—usually someone successful, like the manager of an outstanding football team or the CEO of a large retailer.[11] Often the connotation here is that of a daunting task and a hard act to follow.

John the Baptist is very clear that he is subordinate to Jesus. He is the forerunner, the messenger who prepares. He knows that Jesus, while coming in the prophetic tradition, is not just one in long line of prophets, but one of an altogether different kind, with his own authority and power. He is one who is so different that John declares that he is not worthy to untie his sandals (Mark 1:7), let alone the possibility of passing on some kind of mantle to him.

The prophetic tradition is often critical of those in positions of power and authority. Ezekiel criticises the leaders of Israel for clothing themselves with wool, while not feeding the sheep (Ezek. 34:3). John criticised Herod for his relationship with Herodias, his brother's wife (Matt. 14:3). John also reflects the biblical tradition that prophets don't live in palaces, or in any sort of luxury. They tend to stand outside of the establishment, in the 'wilderness' or 'desert', and critique and challenge from that position.

Jesus challenges the crowds for not recognising who John was and what he represented:

> Jesus began to speak to the crowds about John: 'What did you go out into the wilderness to look at? A reed shaken by the wind? What then did you go out to see? Someone dressed in soft robes? Look, those who put on fine clothing and live in luxury are in royal palaces. What then did you go out to see? A prophet? Yes, I tell you, and more than a prophet. This is the one about whom it is written,
>
> "See, I am sending my messenger ahead of you,
>
> Who will prepare your way before you."
>
> Luke 7:24–27

Jesus is saying that John isn't just any old prophet, but the one previous prophets had spoken about—the forerunner, the path-maker for the Messiah. Jesus is saying, 'If you didn't recognise the significance of this obviously prophetic person, then you don't recognise who I am and what time it is'.[12]

As we have seen, what people wear says something about

their status. We find that when the prodigal son 'came to himself' and returned penitent, his father said, 'Quickly, bring out a robe—the best one—and put it on him; put a ring on his finger and sandals on his feet . . . for this son of mine was dead and is alive again; he was lost and is found'! (Luke 15:22–24). The robe, ring and sandals all indicate the restoration of the status of the son.[13] Interestingly the older son does not raise questions about the clothes his younger brother has been given, but resents the food and the party atmosphere. Maybe both point to his lack of recognition of his own status.

Jesus' coming brings something completely new, not just a slightly different continuation of the old. This is such a radical change that Jesus says:

> No one sews a piece of unshrunk cloth on an old cloak; otherwise, the patch pulls away from it, the new from the old, and a worse tear is made.
>
> Mark 2:21

This new situation is not a patching up, or a dressing up, but a fundamental change. Jesus' life, death and resurrection are not only events in history but themselves together form an eschatological event. Jesus himself brings a completely new situation, which, if we recognise it, brings a complete change of *our* status too. This change of status and of 'being saved' can be expressed in many different ways: sin/redemption; homeless/coming home; exile/return; naked/clothed; flinging off the old and embracing or putting on the new.[14]

An internal relationship with God is marked symbolically and externally by a change of clothes. The change of status is symbolised in baptism by the use of elements of water,

light, oil and clothing.[15] In the early church there is some evidence that believers were baptised naked and this required
the separation of men and women. The deacon or deacon-
ess would strip the candidate and anoint them with the oil
of exorcism, before they were baptised by the Bishop and
anointed with the oil of thanksgiving. They would then put
on white clothes before being led into the assembly of the
faithful.[16]

Coming up out of the water to be re-clothed symbolised
the putting on of the risen Christ, being clothed with the
new humanity. At some point this change of clothing seems
to have been made a more formal symbol by the use of a special garment. We find that a chrism-robe was put on a child
at baptism, as a symbol of the cleansing of sin. Originally
it may have been a cloth put over the head to prevent the
chrism (oil) from being rubbed off. If the child died within
a month of its baptism, the chrisom was used as a shroud;
hence 'chrysom child'.[17]

The tradition of being baptised naked continues to be
practised in the Orthodox church. In western churches in-
fants are often baptised in a white robe, which may be one
handed down for many generations. Adult full immersion
baptisms are often conducted in some form of everyday
clothing which the wearer doesn't mind getting wet.

The underlying symbolism remains the same even if the
individual elements have changed. The change of status is
symbolically expressed and represented at baptism: from nakedness to being clothed; from a state of sin and alienation
to putting on or being covered by God's grace and salvation.
Baptism represents and symbolises who you are—and for
an adult, who you recognise yourself to be—that is, a child

of God.

This union with Christ in baptism is indicated by Paul in a variety of phrases and metaphors to express a deep sense of identification with Christ: 'in Christ', 'into Christ', being 'crucified with Christ', Christ 'living within'. Paul says to the Galatians:

> As many of you as were baptised into Christ have clothed yourselves with Christ.
>
> Gal. 3:27

This can also be translated:

> As many of you who have been baptised into Christ, have put on Christ.[18]

Here Paul uses this language of 'putting on' or 'clothing yourself' with Christ to indicate a believer's change of status. This is an internal and spiritual status, symbolised by, but not given by, physical/material clothes.

In the early churches, questions around social status were unavoidable. Christianity emerged in a highly structured society of powerful/powerless; rich/poor; slave/free. Converts came from each of these groups and this became an issue when they gathered for a common meal. As Paul says, before God, the social class or social status of those who share the bread and wine, those who have been clothed with Christ, count for nothing. This is Paul's theology, but it also has to be said that exactly how that is going to work in practice is not always entirely obvious (1 Cor. 11:33–34).

For a believer, you know who you are, and your identity is in Christ, whatever your outward appearance. People could not identify Jesus by the clothes he was wearing, and generally believers cannot be identified by the clothes they are wearing either. The status of all those who believe, who have been baptised, is the same before God, whatever they are wearing. If we are dressed by someone else, this is something done *to* us. If we accept that 'salvation' is done *to me, for me*, then clothes are symbolically put on *by God*. We accept grace, and God clothes us.

After the specific act of baptism, we return to our normal everyday clothes. The inner and spiritual change is no longer indicated by what we are wearing. This has to be demonstrated in other ways, as we shall see in the next chapter, where 'putting on' is often used as a metaphor for taking on certain virtues or characteristics. Those who have been baptised into Christ's death, have an assurance of life to come— resurrection is in the future, but it spills to the present. Because of Christ's death, our status has changed. Christians share his death and his life, and because the life we now lead is his life, it must be conformed to his. As we will see in the next chapter, this new status has or should have, a significant effect on the way that life is lived.

## Discussion

1. Have you ever worn or been awarded clothing such as a T-shirt or sweatshirt for completing a physical challenge? How does it make you feel when you wear it? How does it make you feel when you see others wearing clothes like this?

2. The character in Jenny Joseph's poem, *When I am an old woman I shall wear purple,* looks forward to having a certain freedom to do whatever she wants, and maybe practising a little now. Does this resonate with you?

3. When you read the stories of Jesus in the gospels, what do you imagine he is wearing, and why?

4. God warns Ezekiel about those who 'take their idols into their hearts'; and Jesus warns that 'no one can serve two masters' (Ezek. 14:4; Matt. 6:24). Think about any possible idols in your life connected with status or clothing. How might you deal with them?

5. How far does having a secure identity in Christ influence (or not) your relationship with clothes and what you wear? And should it?

Only another head
I have, another heart and breast,
Another music, making live, not dead,
Without whom I could have no rest:
In him I am well drest.

*Aaron,* George Herbert (1593—1633)

# 2

## GOODY TWO-SHOES
### *Behaving Well*

The *History of Little Goody Two-shoes* was published in 1765. It is a variation of the Cinderella story. Margery Meanwell is an orphan who is so poor that she only has one shoe. When a rich gentleman gives her a pair of shoes, she is so happy that she goes round telling everyone she has two shoes. She works hard, and in the end marries a rich widower, proving that virtue and hard work will be rewarded, a common theme in children's literature of the time. The phrase, along with being a 'goody-goody', is now often used in a less than flattering way to describe someone perceived to be an excessively or ostentatiously virtuous person, like a teacher's pet.

As Margery shows, the clothes you wear can affect your mental and physical performance. So wearing a red strip can help a team to perform better; the same is true for an individual, such as a boxer or a wrestler. It is not entirely clear whether this enhancement is to do with a self-perception, making you feel more confident, or whether it is a perception of you by others, making them feel less confident; or it may be a combination of both. Apparently in an experiment, putting on a white coat and being told it belonged to a doctor enhanced the performance of one group over another group, who were given the same white coat but were told it belonged to a decorator. This area of research is called 'enclothed cognition', and studies the effects of clothing on cognitive processes.

What you are wearing can affect your performance, as 'Dress for Success' demonstrates. Batman, Superman, Spiderman and Lara Croft wear distinctive clothing to 'save the world'. But do certain types of clothes affect your moral or ethical behaviour? Putting on certain clothes to increase your performance levels, might also involve morally dubious actions in order to achieve the best results for you rather than others, or contributing to the general good.

After many years of struggling with life, several affairs and dabbling in astrology, St. Augustine still felt lost in the middle of all his learning and sensuous living. Partly through the preaching of Bishop Ambrose, he was prepared for baptism on Easter Day in 386. A child's voice, or maybe an angel's, told him to read the scriptures, and the first passage that caught his attention was:

> Let us live honourably as in the day, not in revelling and drunkenness, not in debauchery and licentiousness, not in quarrelling and jealousy. Instead, *put on the Lord Jesus Christ*, and make no provision for the flesh, to gratify its desires.
>
> Rom 13:13, 14.

He went on to say: 'In an instant, as I came to the end of the sentence, it was as though the light of confidence flooded into my heart and all the darkness of doubt was dispelled'.[1]

Augustine here experienced a specific moment of conversion or perhaps the beginnings of a much deeper realisation of God. For him this 'putting on' refers to a specific moment, an identifiable point in time. We saw in the last chapter how a change of status before God can be described as changing from nakedness to being clothed, or by 'putting on' or 'being covered by' God's grace and salvation. Paul expresses this as 'clothing yourself with Christ', or 'putting on Christ' (Gal. 3:27).

Part of Isaiah's good news of deliverance is described in a similar way:

> I will greatly rejoice in the Lord,
> My whole being shall exult in my God;
> For he has clothed me with the garments of
>   salvation,
> He has covered me with the robe of righteousness.

Is. 61:10[2]

Luke's account of Jesus healing the Gerasene demoniac (8:26–39) records a number of contrasts between the man when he was possessed by demons and his situation after Jesus had healed him. Before he met Jesus, amongst other things, he had worn no clothes. After his moment of healing or salvation (the Greek word *sodzo* can mean to heal as well as to save) he was clothed and 'in his right mind'. He is now 'sitting at the feet of Jesus', which is an image of a good disciple who wants to be with Jesus and is willing to learn.

'Putting on' or 'being clothed with' can refer to a specific incident, as we have seen with Augustine and also the demoniac. The language and imagery of 'putting on' or 'being clothed with' can also be used to refer to taking on certain characteristics or virtues. So we find Homer saying that, Achilles leapt among the Trojans, his heart clothed about in might'.[3] By contrast, in the NT, Peter says, 'All of you must clothe yourselves with humility in your dealings with one another' (1 Peter 5:5).

There are many references describing the character of God being clothed with virtues:

Bless the Lord, O my soul.
O Lord my God, you are very great.
You are clothed with honour and majesty,
Wrapped in light as with a garment.

Ps. 104:1; cf 93:1

On the other hand, referring to the wicked:

Therefore pride is their necklace;
Violence covers them like a garment.

Ps. 73:6

The ideal wife is praised as one who has 'strength and dignity' as her clothing (Prov. 31:25).

The 'putting on' of Christ language is a way of describing a spiritual transformation which has a decisive beginning in conversion/baptism, a particular and singular event. Yet this transformation is not complete or final, and so we find the 'putting on' language is also used in relation to virtues or ethical qualities, something on-going, the way the Christian life is exercised and expressed. For human beings, it is part of the nature of characteristics or virtues that they don't come fully packaged and formed. They are not instant or one-off, but rather activities, actions and attitudes which have to be learned, practised and repeated in an on-going way. It is as if you have been given clothes which are too big, and you have to grow into them.

This use of language meaning 'put on' once for all, and 'put on' repeatedly, is worked out in different ways referring to both time and bodies. With reference to time, Christ's death and resurrection was a decisive event, to which believers are joined in baptism. This 'event' is not yet complete, and will not be so until Christ's return. There are various ways of trying to describe this in-between time. Believers' current situation is described in the familiar phrase: 'already and not yet'.

There is a 'sense of already belonging to God's future and needing to learn the habits of heart and life appropriate for it even in the strange present time'.[4] This is one of the reasons why many of Paul's letters are concerned with ethical issues. How should believers behave in this time, in this body? How is faith going to be worked out in the complexities of life—both then and now? What are the rules?

Paul can describe believers as living in the time of the dawning day, as being 'daytime people', 'in the light', but having to live in the darkness of the world (1 Thess. 5:4–10). This naturally has an effect on the way believers should behave:

> But, since we belong to the day, let us be sober and put on the breastplate of faith and love, and for a helmet the hope of salvation.
>
> 1 Thess. 5:8

With reference to bodies, Paul also describes a certain overlapping; an overlap between physical bodies and spiritual bodies. This does not necessarily mean physical now on earth, and spiritual then in heaven; rather 'spiritual' means a body enlivened by God's Spirit (1 Cor. 15:44).[5]

We find that Paul in his letters, uses 'putting on' language in various ways: sometimes referring to time, sometimes to bodies, as well as sometimes meaning to 'put on' once for all, and sometimes to mean 'put on' repeatedly or continuously. Paul often uses 'putting on' language in sections of his letters covering ethical instruction or how to live and exercise the Christian life.

We can see Paul using this 'single event' and 'on-going' 'putting on' language referring to Christian living when writing to the Colossians. So in chapter 3 we find:

> For you *have died*, and your life is hidden with Christ in God. (3:3)

> *Put to death*, therefore, whatever in you is earthly . . . *get rid of* . . . .(3:5, 8)

> Do not lie to one another, seeing that you have *stripped off* the old self with its practices. (3:9)

> . . . and *have clothed* yourselves with the new self, *which is being renewed* in knowledge according to the image of its creator. (3:10)

> As God's chosen ones, holy and beloved, *clothe* yourselves with compassion, kindness, humility, meekness and patience. (3:12)

> Above all, *clothe* yourselves with love, which binds everything together in perfect harmony. (3:14)

Earlier in Colossians, Paul has described Christ as the

'image of the invisible God' (1:15). Believers are being continually transformed into the same image, that of the risen Lord, who is himself the image of God.[6] Col. 3:12 introduces then, not just a string of adjectives chosen at random, but qualities which reflect the nature of the One into whom they have been baptised. So they are to put off, or put to death:

Fornication, impurity, passion, evil desire, greed, anger, wrath, malice, slander, abusive language, lying. (3:5–10)

And instead they are to put on, clothe themselves with:

Compassion, kindness, humility, meekness, patience; bear with one another, forgive each other (as the Lord has forgiven you). (3:12–13)

Paul goes on to say:

Above all, clothe yourselves with love, which binds everything together in perfect harmony. (3:14)

The phrase 'Above all' can have two slightly different meanings. It can mean, put on love *in addition to* all the other virtues, as one which is most important. It could also mean put on love *over everything*, as something which binds together all these virtues—literally an overall. If this 'overall' meaning is taken, this may suggest something more than just an imitation of Christ's conduct, but more of an adoption of his mind as well as his character—'being transformed into his likeness' (2 Cor. 3:18). This transformation is a spiritual and a lifelong exercise.

When doing some random research among friends about

images of clothing in the Bible, one which most people thought of straight away was that of putting on the armour of God (Eph. 6:10–20). This of course is a great Sunday school topic, visually interesting and with a good spiritual message. It is also about transformation.

The message of Ephesians has been summarised as 'sit, walk, stand'.[7] Believers have participated in Christ's victory and have been seated with Christ in the heavenly realms (chapters 1, 2).

> But God, who is rich in mercy, out of the great love with which he loved us even when we were dead through our trespasses, made us alive together with Christ . . . and raised us up with him and *seated* us with him in the heavenly places in Christ Jesus.
>
> Eph. 2:4–6.

This is followed by an appeal to *walk*, that is to live out their status and calling in the world (chapters 3–5).

> And *walk* in love, as Christ loved us. (5:2)

> For once you were darkness, but now you are light in the Lord; *walk* as children of light. (5:8)[8]

And how do you live or 'walk' as children of light? By practising virtues like humility, patience, forgiveness, speaking the truth and exercising self-control.

In the final chapter of the letter, readers are urged to be 'strong in the Lord and in the strength of his power' (6:10). They are urged to 'put on' or 'take up' the whole armour of God (6:11, 13). This is a spiritual armour: *fasten* the belt of truth, *put on* the breastplate of righteousness, *put on* shoes 'ready to proclaim the gospel of peace', *take* the shield of faith, the helmet of salvation and the sword of the Spirit, not forgetting to 'pray in the Spirit at all times'. Three times they are urged to *stand*, to maintain their position of victory as they live out their lives in the world.

> Put on the whole armour of God, so that you may be able to *stand* . . . and having done everything, to *stand* firm. *Stand* therefore . . . .
>
> Eph 6:11, 13, 14

Here is a realistic perspective on Christian existence, not an effortless or trouble-free assignment. Humanity is very vulnerable to the forces of evil, death and destruction. If believers are to stand firm in this battle, they will need divine protection and equipping. The armour is not just any old armour, but specifically the armour *of God*, because the battle is against the 'spiritual forces of evil'.

It has often been suggested that Paul was looking at the dress of his Roman guard while writing these words, and taking the imagery from there. This may have provided part of the background, but such armour imagery and vocabulary has a much wider history.

This is what Isaiah says about the coming Messiah:

> Righteousness shall be the belt around his waist
> And faithfulness the belt around his loins.
>
> Is. 11:5

And of God himself:

> He put on righteousness like a breastplate,
>   And a helmet of salvation on his head;

He put on garments of vengeance for clothing,
And wrapped himself in fury as in a mantle.

Is. 59:17

The Lord will take his zeal as his whole armour,
And will arm all creation to repel his enemies;
He will put on righteousness as a breastplate,
And wear impartial justice as a helmet;
He will take holiness as an invincible shield,
    and sharpen stern wrath for a sword.

Wisdom 5:17–20

Paul encourages believers in Rome to 'put on the armour of light'; and those in Thessalonia, to be self-controlled: 'put on the breastplate of faith and love, and for a helmet the hope of salvation' (Rom. 13:12; 1 Thess. 5:8).

The passage in Ephesians 6 teaches us that the world is not a neutral place. The language used may seem poetic and symbolic to us, but says that there is a battle going on between good and evil. We need to receive support as well as take action to make sure that we don't get caught up in the battle on the wrong side.

For all of us, quite a bit of the time, life is a battle—a battle to keep going under pressure, coping with tragedy or disloyalty, coping with sin and temptation or just life in general. It can be a battle to maintain an appropriate lifestyle in society. We can all get set in our ways or like to follow a routine, without realising it. We get dressed in a certain order, and if we do it differently, it doesn't feel right—just try putting the opposite leg in your trousers first.

Having 'put on' Christ at baptism, and knowing that we 'sit in heavenly places' with Christ, we are called to live a life as befits our new status. We are, in some sense, caught up in the narrative of both Christ's death, and also of his resurrection. We are called to develop our Christian character, putting it on with conscious thought and effort. The more we exercise and demonstrate these qualities, the more we are enabled to stand, and the closer to Christ we become; and the closer to Christ we become, the more we are able to stand in battles. These are mutually reinforcing. Moral activity is not just a chore and a bore, but itself gives us protection. We don't always need to be challenged to 'fight harder', but to focus more on Christ (Phil. 3:12).

Yet it is often a lifestyle which can model our beliefs in a much more powerful way than anything we may say. It is hard to speak of God with any conviction if we claim to follow Jesus and do not try to demonstrate an appropriate lifestyle. We don't need literally to fight, but attributes of truth, righteousness, justice, peace, faith and prayer do not necessarily come naturally or easily. They are certainly not soft options.

We are not just trying to be better people or to do things differently, maybe more lovingly, just because we think it's a good idea. The reason we do it is because our changed status means we have a new way of being in the world. We have a status which needs to be exercised, learned, nurtured and developed, formed and shaped; and above all, practised. We need to grow in holiness.

> You were taught to put away (or put off) your former way of life, your old self, corrupt and deluded by its lusts, and to be renewed in the spirit of your minds, and to clothe yourselves with the new self, created

according to the likeness of God in true righteousness
and holiness.

Eph. 4:22–24

Putting on certain clothes can make us *feel* different; in a
similar way, putting on other clothes can make us *act* differently. Certain clothes demonstrate *outwardly* what is going
on *inwardly*. Conversely, bad behaviour which brings disre-
spect is not worthy of our 'uniform' (see Mark 12:38–40).
It's very difficult to make yourself act in a certain way solely
though willpower or head knowledge. Moral action needs
to be the result of something else, as fruit is a clear demon-
stration of the nature of the tree which bore it (see Matt.
7:16, 20).[9]

The casting off of the old person, putting on a new person,
is not the same as casting off one's old bad character, and
putting on the new Christian character. That new character is not fully formed and we are not instantly changed
into an ideal person, or perhaps a saint. Unfortunately not.
We are not to be transformed into what we think we *should
be*, but into the likeness of Christ. Sadly, this is not effort
free, and we need to work at it. 'Clothes don't just fall out
of the wardrobe and put themselves on you; you have to
think about what you're going to wear'.[10] Yet we are not on
our own. Our human responsibility to address behaviour is
combined with a divine enabling as part of the work of the
Holy Spirit, described by Luke in terms of an 'enclothing'
(Luke 24:49; cf. 2 Chron. 24:20).

There is a sense in which when we put on clothes we
become another person. We can also take on attitudes that
those clothes represent. Clothes affect our behaviour; they

can make us feel different, or they may give us more confidence. The trouble is, of course, we can put on all the fine clothes we want, and they can remain a covering.

We take off and put on clothes; they get dirty and wear out; they need washing and replacing, changing and renewing. In a similar way, we need constantly to be 'putting on', renewing, enhancing, deepening, positive ethical qualities and actions. Otherwise the clothes we put on will remain a covering and won't reflect any change going on inside and underneath.

Perhaps when we think or are tempted to think what we show on the outside is 'real', then we are in trouble. If you know you are clothed with Christ, and are being transformed into his likeness, even very slowly, this is the kind of clothing that gives assurance and confidence. We are still in some sense the same person. We have a new language and understanding, a new identity, but at the core, remain the *person*, precious and full of promise. We cannot pray ourselves to become someone else, but we are called and being transformed. We act differently when wearing different clothes. We want to let Jesus do the same.

## Discussion

1. Does wearing different clothing make you act in a different way? What might this represent? Can you think of any examples?

2. How do you feel about wearing badges, in the form of ribbons, wristbands, red noses, or clothes in pink, or Jeans for Genes? How far has it become necessary to be *seen* to support causes; something worn to 'raise awareness' and to 'show we care'?

3. How far do we live in God as we live in our favourite clothes?

4. Sins are often not something dramatic, but more of a drift in a certain direction, perhaps like clothes gradually getting dirty or becoming more worn. Positively, fruits also develop gradually. Think about and share anything that helps you remain alert to both these possibilities.

5. In a world where many don't have adequate clothing, how can you remind yourself to thank God for what you have? Why not challenge yourself to thank God for each item of clothing you put on over the next seven days.

Let holy charity
mine outward vesture be,
and lowliness become mine inner clothing;
true lowliness of heart,
which takes the humbler part,
and o'er its own shortcomings weeps with loathing.
    *Come down, O love divine*, trans. R.F. Littledale (1833–1890)

# 3

## I'M NOT GOING OUT DRESSED LIKE THIS!
### *Being Naked Before God*

Turning up somewhere in the wrong clothes is something we probably all try to avoid. 'I didn't get the memo' usually means 'nobody told me what to wear'. Wearing the wrong clothes can be embarrassing; wearing no clothes at all is probably a hundred times worse, as evidenced by recurring nightmares of being naked in the street. One of the main functions of clothes is to prevent us from being naked, that is, unclothed. We are born naked, but actually spend most of our lives clothed or covered in some way. Human beings are in fact the only creatures to wear clothes and the only ones ashamed of being naked.

Physically, clothing offers protection to our bodies from assaults of the weather and disease. It also provides us with some form of modesty. Protection and modesty vary considerably depending on social and climatic preferences. On the whole, nakedness is seen as something to be avoided. Being naked comes about for various reasons and at different times. It can be something we choose to do, as in naturism; it can be something we have little option about—taking a bath or visiting the doctor. It can happen against our will, through poverty, oppression or madness. For many, the experience of nakedness may be something fairly fleeting—a short moment between the shower and breakfast.

We usually get ourselves dressed. One way of exercising control over another or if you want to humiliate your enemies, is to deprive them of clothing. Prisoners are strip searched; denial of clothing represents a stripping of identity, of power and of honour. The power of an oppressor can be used in this way to punish, humiliate, degrade and shame their victims. All these elements are of course in play at Jesus' crucifixion.[1]

The first mention of nakedness in the Bible is a positive one (Gen. 2:25). In the Garden of Eden, 'the man and his wife were both naked, and were *not* ashamed'. Being naked is a very prominent feature of the second creation story (2:25; 3:21). It seems that nakedness is being used symbolically here, as part of a much bigger picture, meaning something much more than no clothes. Although the story does not say anything specific about their life before something happened, there is a harmony here between creation and man and woman; things are right with God in a relationship of trust and openness, with no guilt or shame.

But something happened, something went wrong. Adam and Eve then knew they were naked, covered themselves with leaves and tried to hide.[2] In response to God's question, 'Where are you'? Adam replies, 'I heard the sound of you in the garden, and I was afraid, because I was naked; and I hid myself'. God asks, 'Who told you that you were naked'?

Adam and Eve are not just covering their private parts with fig leaves, as portrayed in paintings and cartoons. They could perhaps have covered their whole bodies with cloaks

of leaves. They were trying to hide from God in the trees—
to hide all of themselves completely. God asks, 'Where are
you'? not 'Why are you wearing leaves'? It's not really a question of God needing to know where they are exactly. God's
question reflects something much broader and more significant than being temporarily lost. If all is well, why are Adam
and Eve hiding?

'Nakedness' is being used symbolically here to demonstrate that relationships have changed, and are sadly broken.
This is Adam and Eve's relationship with God, between
themselves, and with the natural world. As John Goldingay
notes: 'But we were never supposed to be afraid of the one
who wants to go for a walk with us'.[3]

At the end of this story, at the moment when Adam and
Eve are sent out of the garden, God provides a means of
healing what is broken. God himself 'made garments of
skins for the man and for his wife, and clothed them' (3:21).
Significantly, these are *provided by God*.

After the creation stories in Genesis 1–3, the OT reflects
an instinctive dislike of nakedness, which was a matter of
deep shame and distress. The two main reasons for being
naked were because you were poor or because your enemy
was humiliating you. So we read that if a cloak is taken as
a pledge, then it must be returned by sunset, 'for it may be
your neighbour's only clothing to use as a cover; in what else
shall that person sleep'? (Ex. 22:26). Job says that the poor
and needy 'lie all night, naked, without clothing, and having
no covering in the cold' (Job 24:7; also 22:6; 24:7, 10).

The practice of stripping a defeated enemy was something
done literally and was also a vivid symbol of their complete
humiliation.[4] Hanum, king of the Ammonites, sent David's

envoys back humiliated: He 'shaved off half the beard of each, cut off their garments in the middle at their hips, and sent them away' (NIV: *at the buttocks*). The men were greatly ashamed, and David told them to stay in Jericho until their beards had grown again (2 Sam. 10:4–6). As a prophetic symbol, Isaiah apparently went about with no clothes or shoes for three years—a symbol of dominance for the victor and humiliation and shame for the defeated (Is. 20:3–4).[5]

Nakedness indicated both poverty and powerlessness. Conversely, the provision of clothing for others indicated, not only a loving concern and care, but also reflected a moral obligation towards them. God says,

> Is not this the fast that I choose . . .
> Is it not to share your bread with the hungry,
> And bring the homeless poor into your house;
> When you see the naked, to cover them,
> And not to hide yourself from your own kin?
>
> Is. 58:7[6]

Nakedness and clothing are very strong images and are often used to convey significant symbolic meaning and importance. Those coming before a holy and majestic God are to be correctly dressed. Even God's heavenly attendants, the seraphim, are covered, and this is part of a proper reverence in God's presence (Is. 6:2).[7] In particular, priests are not to be naked before God. We find elaborate instructions for Aaron and his sons' priestly clothes, including special linen undergarments to cover 'the hips to the thighs' (Ex. 28–29; 39; esp. 28:42; 39:28).

The metaphor of God clothing nakedness is used to show

God's great love for his people. If being clothed by God symbolises his love for his people, conversely nakedness can be used as an expression of God's judgement, especially on the arrogance of Israel. Nakedness as an exposure of the most shameful kind is a sign of or a call for divine judgement. Clothing/love and nakedness/judgement are explored particularly in Hosea and Ezekiel.

There are many references to 'uncovering the nakedness of' in the law code in Leviticus (18, 20), and here this has the meaning of sexual relations.[8] This covering and uncovering of nakedness referring to the most intimate loving relationship, is found in the extended metaphor in the book of Hosea, where God's relations with Israel are depicted as being like those between a husband and wife. God loved her/Israel so much that he gave her extensive gifts, and saved her from shame by clothing her nakedness (Hosea 2:5, 8).

But Israel was unfaithful, committing adultery by worshipping foreign gods, 'when God will now withdraw his protection', and 'uncover her shame':

Therefore I will take back
  my grain in its time,
  and my wine in its season;
And I will take away my wool and my flax,
  which were to cover her nakedness.
Now I will uncover her shame
  in the sight of her lovers,
  and no one shall rescue her out of my hand. . .
I will punish her for the festival days of the Baals,
  when she offered incense to them
And decked herself with her ring and jewellery,

and went after her lovers,
and forgot me, says the Lord.

Hos. 2:9, 10, 13

Ezekiel describes God's tender care for Jerusalem. He rescued her from being abandoned at birth; he cared for her as she grew up, but still being 'naked and bare', provided care and tenderness for her, including clothing of 'fine linen, rich fabric, and embroidered cloth', so that she grew 'exceedingly beautiful' (16:13).

This depiction of God's love, care and attention is set in the context of God's judgement on Jerusalem and her 'abominations'. God goes on to say, in spite of all this generous care and provision:

> But you trusted in your beauty, and played the whore because of your fame . . . You took some of your garments, and made for yourself colourful shrines, and on them played the whore.

Ezek. 16:15, 16

Elsewhere, the city of Jerusalem, or the nation as a whole, is often depicted as a 'wanton woman':

The Lord said:
Because the daughters of Zion are haughty
  and walk with outstretched necks,
  glancing wantonly with their eyes,
  mincing along as they go,
  tinkling with their feet;
The Lord will afflict with scabs
  the heads of the daughters of Zion,

and the Lord will lay bare their secret parts.

Is. 3:16, 17[9]

The next verses continue this theme, and also provide us with an informative insight into the clothing fashions of the day:

> On that day the Lord will take away the finery of the anklets, the headbands, and the crescents; the pendants, the bracelets, and the scarves; the head-dresses, the armlets, the sashes, the perfume boxes, and the amulets; the signet rings and nose-rings; the festal robes, the mantles, the cloaks and the handbags; the garments of gauze, the linen garments, the turbans, and the veils.

Is. 3:18–23

We have seen how images of nakedness can symbolise God's judgement, and images of God clothing symbolise his love. Yet there is also a sense in which if we are to have an intimate relationship with God and allow God to love us, we have to be exposed before him. Stripping is not as easy as it sounds, but this is something, in a symbolic and spiritual sense, which we have to be willing to let happen. In the presence of God, all symbolic layers of dirt and grime in the form of habits, preferences, pretences and falsehood need to be stripped away. Symbolically, there is a sense in which, when we are fully and completely open and receptive to God, we are naked, because we have stripped off all of that which we hide behind. We cannot pretend to be someone else while we are naked. We have to be willing to become naked before God in order that he may clothe us.

Sadly there is a need to do this stripping off more than

once—in fact, often. This is not an automatic, simple or painless process, as C.S. Lewis' character, Eustace, discovered.[10] Eustace who is cowardly and vain, finds himself turned into a dragon which was 'very dreary'. Bit by bit he discovers the pleasure both of being liked and of liking other people—something quite new to him. He meets Aslan who takes him to a big well or bath full of clear, bubbling water, and tells him to undress. Eustace begins to pull off his dragon scales, and then his whole skin peels off, 'as if I was a banana'. As he put his feet in the water, he sees that they are wrinkled and scaly just as they had been before. He peels off that skin, but as he puts his feet in the water, the same thing happens again, and again. Then Aslan says, "You will have to let me undress you." Aslan's claws 'hurt worse than anything I've ever felt', and the final skin was thicker, darker and more knobbly than the others. Aslan throws him into the well where Eustace realises he is a boy again. The lion then dresses him himself and returns him to the others.

There are obvious baptismal images here, but the dynamic is also significant. It was only through a very dreary time as a dragon that Eustace discovered something about who he was. He cannot escape Aslan's call or gaze, and does what he says. But in the end it is only Aslan who can undress him fully, and it hurts. It is only Aslan who can re-clothe him. As Rowan Williams points out, this rediscovery of our human identity is not something we can do in our own strength. We will always be tempted to stop before we get to the deepest level, because it hurts. 'Only Aslan's claws can strip away the entire clothing of falsehood with which we have surrounded ourselves'. He goes on to say that what is required is not that we go bravely on in our own strength exploring our ego, 'only that we declare to God our willingness to be stripped'.[11]

This 'stripping' is not the same as trying to find who or what we are 'under the skin'. A certain amount of self-awareness and self-examination is good, but an obsession with being 'true to yourself' and finding your 'real self' can become a pointless exercise, when in reality, there is probably no such thing to be found. We are ourselves in the layers. There can be a danger of substituting self-understanding for actual change. For believers, a God-shaped hole in the centre, needs to be filled by God, grounded in the love of Christ.[12] The only thing we need to do is declare to God our willingness to be stripped. When held before God right self-knowledge becomes a profound act of humility and worship.

Saint Francis acted out this metaphor when announcing his betrothal to Lady Poverty, by publicly stripping off his clothing and flinging it at the feet of his protesting father and the local bishop. Ruth Burrows, writing about life as a Carmelite sister, describes the 'essence' of Carmel as "the poor ones standing nakedly exposed to God, with nothing to offer him but their need and emptiness".[13]

This concept of 'exposure' before God is echoed by Jean Vanier in his work with 'abled' and 'disabled' people living in community. He argues that exposing ourselves to a physical, emotional and spiritual nakedness is what makes us human. He sees our neediness, not only as a fact of life, but also as a gift that orients us and our freedom toward others.[14] This recognition of being 'naked' with those with disabilities is also recognised by Henri Nouwen when he first went to work at a *L'Arche* community. He says he felt naked, because his past achievements (as a priest, an eminent lecturer, an academic, an author) were not recognised, or seen to be of any importance at all.[15]

All this stripping can sound quite negative and suggests some kind of submission to another—a kind of surrender of control, something passive.[16] And this is what it is. But when that surrender is to the God who loves us, this becomes something for our good, and we can then become clothed *by God*, as we saw was the case in Genesis. As a baby or child is dressed by its parents, so being clothed by God is one aspect of 'becoming like a child of God'.

We see this in the parable of the Loving Father/Prodigal Son (Luke 15:11–32). 'Dying of hunger' the son 'came to himself' and went home; but it is the father who clothes him. In the parable of the Good Samaritan, the traveller is stripped and beaten, rescued and clothed by an outsider, which is often seen as symbolic of Christ himself (Luke 10:29–37).

This stripping of ourselves before God needs to take place on some kind of regular basis (every day, weekly, before or part of a church service, a quiet day, a week of retreat etc). The result, knowing that we are being clothed by God, means that we can have a different kind of relationship with our bodies and ourselves. We do not need to strive for the perfect body beautiful, so much played on by advertisements for particular clothing and products. Yes, we need to respect, exercise and not abuse our bodies, but knowing that we have been clothed by God enables us to be more ease with ourselves.

This lack of worry about clothes or the lack of them is reflected in C.S. Lewis' description of heaven in *The Great*

*Divorce*. Not long after his arrival,

> I saw people coming to meet us . . . Some were na-
> ked, some robed. But the naked ones did not seem less
> adorned, and the robes did not disguise . . .

This theme is picked up again later with the arrival of the
'saint' Sarah Smith:

> I cannot now remember whether she was naked or cloth-
> ed . . . For clothes in that country are not a disguise.[17]

Part of the repeated message to the seven churches in Revelation 2 and 3 is to recognise the voice of Christ calling them
to repentance, and to do so before it is too late. There is also
a repeated call to individual believers to 'conquer', that is,
stand firm in the battle against temptation and persecution.
The future reward for those who stand firm to the end is described using a rich imagery, including that of clothing.

> Yet you have still a few people in Sardis who have not
> soiled their clothes; they will walk with me, dressed in
> white, for they are worthy. If you conquer, you will be
> clothed like them in white robes and I will not blot your
> name out of the book of life.
>
> Rev. 3:4

> For you say, "I am rich, I have prospered, and I need
> nothing." You do not realize that you are wretched, piti-
> able, poor, blind, and naked. Therefore I counsel you
> to buy from me gold refined by fire so that you may
> be rich; and white robes to clothe you and to keep the
> shame of your nakedness from being seen; and salve to

anoint your eyes so that you may see.

Rev. 3:17, 18

Or as *The Message* version says: 'Buy your clothes from me, clothes designed in Heaven'. As in Genesis, so here in Revelation, the clothes to cover nakedness are to be provided by God.

Naked I came from my mother's womb, and naked shall I return there; the Lord gave and the Lord has taken away; blessed be the name of the Lord.

Job 1:21; cf. Eccls. 5:15

This verse, familiar from funeral services, comes after Job has lost everything: livestock, servants, sons, daughters, house. He is now without possessions, protection and security. We arrive in this world literally naked, unprotected and helpless, and while we may not all die naked, there is a sense in which 'we can't take it with us' and are forced to return to God without anything.

We have a great capacity to hide our true selves. There is a sense in which, in order to move closer to God, we have to make ourselves naked, vulnerable and exposed before Him, before we are able to accept His love and forgiveness. This is not something forced upon us by God as oppressor, exercising control, but as part of a loving relationship. It may not always be an entirely pleasant experience, as we gradually peel away layers before his gaze, but we do this in the secure knowledge of his love, and so that he can shape us to become more like him. We are not naked before God so that he can humiliate and shame us, but so that he can clothe us. And nothing can separate us from the love of Christ.[18]

## Discussion

1.  Have you ever had a dream where you were naked in
    public? How do you think you might react if you had
    such a dream?
2.  Think of someone who regularly dresses well with 'not a
    hair out of place'. How does that make you feel?
3.  How far do you think the kinds of clothes people wear
    is a barrier to getting to know them? How do you think
    your choice of clothes affects the way people respond
    to you?
4.  Do you find the symbolism of being naked before God
    helpful? If so, why? If not, why do you think that might
    be? Are other images more helpful to you?
5.  What practices might be helpful in stripping away our
    strengths and weaknesses before God? What helps you
    to bring your whole undefended self before God?

Nothing in my hand I bring,
simply to the cross I cling;
naked, come to thee for dress;
helpless, look to thee for grace;
foul, I to the fountain fly;
wash me, Saviour, or I die.

*Rock of Ages,* Augustus M. Toplady (1740–1778)

# 4

## PUT ON THE STRIP AND JOIN THE CLUB
### *Kinship and Belonging*

In December 2015, a temporary worker, Nicola Thorp, 27, was sent home from her assigned job as a receptionist at a leading London firm for refusing to wear shoes with a 2 to 4in heel. In a court case she argued that the company could not give her a reason as to why wearing flat shoes would impair her from doing her job to a high standard.

In May 2014, students at Wasatch High School in the Mormon state of Utah, found that photos in the 2014 yearbook had been edited—adding sleeves, raising necklines and removing tattoos. Students protested that the school's actions were inappropriate in the 'land of the free'; the school said students had been warned that photos might be edited to correct 'violation'.

Apparently the first seven seconds of an encounter are critical in terms of the image we convey. This is the length of time it takes for someone to assess your clothes and personal style, as to who you are and what you care about. For businesses, it is therefore very important that what employees wear reflects the business accurately, and a dress code can help to ensure that. The question becomes, as illustrated by the 'heels' incident, how far can a rigid dress code be enforced when this does not involve other issues, such as that of personal safety?

Appraising individuals and groups by what they are wearing is not something new. In theory, Roman society was founded on clear distinctions of status which determined political rights and social standing. Society was stratified between citizen and non-citizen, between free and slave. Slavery seems to have become a focus for anxieties about wider changes in the social structure, as society became stratified by wealth and power rather than the distinction between citizen and non-citizen. So Pliny notes that 'The estate manager should be as near as possible to his master in intelligence, but not think himself so'.[1]

In the city of Rome there was an elaborate system of status-based attire, distinguishing those of high social standing and wealth (*honestiores*) and those of lower classes (*humiliores*). There was no form of dress specifically for slaves, and neither were there clear physical differences between slaves and slave-owners. This meant it was not always possible to identify one's supposed inferiors in the street. In order to distinguish between the two classes, there was a formal proposal in the Senate to make slaves wear distinctive clothing. However, this was rejected on the grounds that slaves would then realise just how many of them there were, and they would be quite likely to join together in rebellion against their owners.[2]

Making your slaves dress in a certain way would be a forceful and psychological way of enforcing and reinforcing dominance by one group over another. Prisoners are often forced to wear prison clothes as a form of oppression, as in striped pyjamas or orange jumpsuits.[3]

More positively, clothing does provide a strong expressed sense of community, a bond of fellowship with others. Supporters of a particular football team share a bond together by wearing the team strip. School uniform can provide an identity and be something in which pupils can take pride. Companies often do have a written or unwritten dress code. If you want people to value the work they do, taking pride in appearance and making an effort can transmit a powerful message.

Over the years Christian groups have often been identified by the particular kind of clothes they wear, from the habits of monks and nuns, to dog collars, and the distinctive dress of Amish and Brethren groups. Rumer Godden writes about making a Solemn Profession in a Benedictine convent:

> On the evening before it she would go to the chapter house where there would be two tables; on one the ring, cowl and mitra (crown) would be laid out; on the other the clothes she had come in, her last worldly clothes. . . In front of all the nuns (she) would have to go up and lay her hand on one table or the other.[4]

Sister Rosemary (Community of the Holy Name, Derby) notes how the expression 'taking the veil' describing the entry of a woman into a religious community is no longer so appropriate, since the veil is now hardly worn at all. The ceremony for receiving a novice has usually been called 'clothing' since it is still marked by the wearing of the habit for the first time. But of course the promises of commitment are far more important. She describes how, in earlier times, when the novitiate was very large, a number of charges had come in with a romantic picture of themselves looking holy in a habit, and being effortlessly sanctified. Once they had received the coveted garments, and found themselves absorbed in the unglamorous routine of convent life, they thought better of it, and soon left. 'Partly because of this high rate of early departure, many of us, over the years, have been 'clothed' in a second-hand habit—a salutary reminder that the real work is only just beginning'.[5]

Distinctive clothing not only makes you part of a community, but it can also provide a strong sense of differentiation from the 'other'. On Jacob's return to Bethel, the place where he had met with God, Jacob says to his household and to all who were with him:

> Put away the foreign gods that are among you, and purify yourselves, and change your clothes; then come, let us to up the Bethel, that I may make an altar there to the God who answered me in the day of my distress and has been with me wherever I have gone.
>
> Gen. 35:2

Changing clothes here is seen as part of a purification from things 'foreign'. This may be 'changing' in the sense of putting on clean clothes, but may also well have been a literal putting away of 'foreign' clothes, perceived to be part of an identity with a foreign culture and foreign gods. The people give Jacob all the foreign gods and earrings they had, and he buried them. The text does not tell us what they put on instead, but this may have been some kind of acceptable clothing to the group, signifying their identification with the group and separation from those outside.

Clothing provides a strong sense of group identity. This means that any deviation from an acceptable group dress code comes to be seen, not only as a lack of commitment to the group, but as a deviation from the fundamental beliefs of the group, along with moral deviance and a lack of commitment to God.

Hudson Taylor (1832–1905) faced opposition and criticism from some fellow missionaries when he adopted local Chinese dress and grew his hair into a long plait (*bianzi*). He did it to identify better with the local Chinese people he loved and with whom he wanted to share God's love. Others, especially those at his mission headquarters in London, saw his actions as a dilution of the Christian message and an indication of identification with a pagan culture.

> A belief in the equality of all men before God, too literally acted upon, can produce patterns of behaviour which no imperial society can accept with equanimity. To the *taipans* and all the other people who believed that the white man's dignity rested in strict adherence to British dress and British habits, Hudson Taylor's action was deeply shocking. He had gone native. He had lost face. He had broken the magic ring of white solidarity. The word *traitor* was not too harsh to describe him.[6]

Later, when Hudson Taylor founded his own mission society, the China Inland Mission, he set out the distinctive features of the Mission, including its inter-denominational nature, no guaranteed salaries, no direct fund raising, along with:

> Sixth, as a courtesy to the Chinese people, the missionaries

would wear Chinese clothes and worship in buildings
built in the Chinese style.[7]

Enforcing a strict dress code can be used by those in positions of leadership as a controlling mechanism to dictate
what is acceptable. Often, since men tended to be in leadership positions, it was they who decided what was acceptable
for their women to wear. This was particularly noticeable in
the Amish and Mennonite communities in North America,
arriving from Europe from the mid-1700s onwards.

> When they first settled there, the main stress was on
> simplicity, nonconformity and modesty. This did not
> result in a standard form of dress, but in plain and un-
> adorned clothing reflecting contemporary peasant style.
> As these groups' identities began to be threatened by in-
> creased interchange with the 'world', emphasis on spe-
> cific modes of dress began to surface. Leaders, sensing a
> breakdown, began reaching for ways to reinforce their
> groups' identities. Many Swiss German groups felt it
> important to outline specific styles to keep their people
> separate from the world, nonconformed and humble.[8]

For Mennonite women in Canada, this standard of noncon-
formity was particularly gender specific in the issue of dress.
Dress that was perceived to be too fashionable or immodest
was linked to the fall and satanic, sexual temptation. Some
women 'rested in the security of the uniform conformity . . .
others wrestled deeply with wrenching bitterness' over such
matters as covered heads, closed-toes shoes and prohibitions
against lipstick. Wives of clergymen were usually the first
ones called to comply with standards of conformity. So in

1898 a Mrs Wismer was told that she must wear plain dress and not wear her beads and jewellery, or her newly ordained husband would not be allowed to preach.[9]

Head covering was to be worn by all baptised women, following 1 Cor. 11:3–6 (cf. 1 Tim. 2:9; 1 Peter 3:3). This rule, along with other dress regulations, was encoded in church statutes, and was made a test of church membership. Dress regulations concerning head covering caused acrimonious debate and conflict especially within Swiss Mennonite communities in Ontario. Should the wearing of a bonnet, enclosing back of the head and tied under chin, be enforced, or could this be replaced by a more modern hat?

Susannah Cressman's diary entries reflect the conflict:

1915: 'went to church; Jacob Schmidt preached sermon on bonnet question, took vote on same'

1918: 'meeting at our church to consider bonnet question and some other minor troubles'

1922: 'ministers and bishops met at the church to thresh out the bonnet trouble here—had a three day session'

1923: 'Went to conference all day—discussion on bonnet question'[10]

The 'bonnet question' led to a church split centring on differing interpretations of scripture, and divergent views about a woman's place in relation to God and man. The new church developed a reputation as 'liberal', being one in which women were allowed to be members of the church council and participate in decision making. The changing role of women in the early twentieth century in higher education and professions such as nursing and teaching, meant that some no longer wanted to carry the badge of noncon-formity for the entire church community, or have their role strictly defined. The wearing of a bonnet declined signifi-cantly in the 1940s, but head-covering remained a sign of a woman's church membership well into the 1960s, and for some communities continues today. In some more tradi-tional groups, men also adhere to church prescribed dress standards, and women may still cover their heads in defer-ence to the hierarchical order of God-Christ-man-woman.

Positively, the effect of wearing the same kind of clothes can result in a strong sense of group identity. The uniformi-ty that results from adherence to a dress code also promotes group unity, identity and sameness. More negatively, con-trol of what is to be worn can enable group leaders to exert authority over its members. Issues over clothing raise ques-tions about how a group controls its membership, and at what point does exclusion become a distinct possibility, or even a reality.

Controlling membership of your group is not a new issue. Matthew was probably writing his gospel in the context of a small group of Christians in fierce dispute with Judaism, so these words of Jesus would be particularly relevant:

> Beware of false prophets, who come to you in sheep's clothing but inwardly are ravenous wolves. You will know them by their fruits.
>
> Matt. 7:15

He is obviously aware of the threat to his community from 'false prophets' (mentioned again in 24:11), although who they were is not specified. 'A wolf in sheep's clothing' sug-gests an outward appearance of conformity to group norms, even warmth and protection, but concealing an inner, hidden deceit or disguised lack loyalty; a contrast between inward intention and outward appearance.[11] An outer covering may hide an inner intention to challenge, to disrupt or to eat and destroy. It is possible to tell who they are by looking at their 'fruits', their deeds; this is how they will be known. What they do has to be in accord with the will of God, which, for Matthew, is exercised by hearing and doing the words of Jesus (7:24).

The concept and imagery of inclusion or exclusion, depending on what you are wearing, is also found later in Matthew's gospel in the parable of the King's Banquet or Wedding Feast (22:1–10). It seems that Matthew, or his tradition, may have attached a short piece to the main parable (22:11–14). This is about the man who is not wearing an appropriate wedding garment, and who is then bound and thrown into outer darkness.

The king, coming to see his guests, 'noticed a man there who was not wearing a wedding robe'. This man stands out as one not dressed for the occasion, which is insulting both to the king and the occasion. He says, "Friend, how did you get in here without a wedding robe?"

The word 'friend' only occurs three times in Matthew (here; 20:13, labourers in the vineyard; and 26:50, Judas' betrayal). Each time the word is used it suggests that the speaker knows that the addressee has done something else wrong or offensive. So the labourers were grumbling about the terms they had previously agreed. Judas tried to greet Jesus with a kiss, but has previously agreed his betrayal. What then has this man done wrong, symbolised by not wearing wedding clothes? It could be that he has not been doing good deeds which follow Jesus' teaching. Another possibility could be that he has not been invited.

Although this sounds shocking to us, it reflects the fact that it is God who does the inviting. The whole parable puts the emphasis on God's gracious initiative to call those he wishes. This is a parable about the Kingdom of Heaven and the judgement and division it brings (22:2, 13, 14). This is Matthew's way of emphasising the role and gift of God's grace. You can receive God's invitation and turn it down; you can receive God's invitation and accept; but you can't turn up without an invitation at all. It is God's grace which ultimately creates kinship and it is this which clothes believers appropriately.

A similar understanding of God's grace is reflected earlier in Matthew's parable chapter (13). There we find that it is God himself who gives or withholds seeing/hearing/understanding, so that people may or may not turn to him (see also Is. 6:8–13, where the prophet's commission is to go and preach to a people who will not understand). As found elsewhere in Matthew, who is 'in' and who is 'out' is not for us to know or decide; the weeds and the wheat 'grow together until the harvest' (13:30).[12] God is judge and he will sort it out in the end. Those who consider themselves to be on the 'inside' should be both living by and sharing this grace.

This theme of being invited to a wedding banquet is also found in Revelation where the feast is the eschatological wedding feast of Jesus Messiah. 'Blessed are those who are invited to the marriage supper of the Lamb' (Rev 19:9).

'Let us rejoice and exult
  And give him the glory,

> For the marriage of the Lamb has come,
>   And his bride has made herself ready;
> To her it has been granted to be clothed
>   With fine linen, bright and pure'
> - for the fine linen is the righteous deeds of the saints
>
> Rev. 19:7, 8.

The book of Revelation is addressed to those currently undergoing persecution, and a strong visual image for the righteous who overcome is the promise of wearing fine white linen. John, in the Spirit, writes to the people of Sardis:

> Yet you have still a few people in Sardis who have not soiled their clothes; they will walk with me, dressed in white, for they are worthy. If you conquer, you will be clothed like them in white robes and I will not blot your name out of the book of life
>
> Rev. 3:4, 5; also 3:18

In times of persecution these images give a strong sense of comfort to individuals as well as encouraging cohesion as a group. So for the readers of both Matthew and Revelation, threats posed by hostile outsiders are partly answered by a doctrine of reward and punishment: their troubles will not be in vain, and the rewards are great.

We have seen how the wearing of a particular type of clothing often carries with it a strong sense of group identity. Clothing creates community. At the same time it also creates borders and boundaries. We can also see how encouraging modesty which reflects a thoughtfulness about your clothes, is different from a call for modesty that is really an excuse for one individual or group to exercise control over another.[13]

A change of status at conversion/baptism, is not just something for an individual, but also has a communal dimension. An individual relates to God, but also to the wider Christian community. On the one hand, we can choose what we want to wear from a vast available range, and we can be quite individualistic about our style. On the other hand, we need to dress appropriately for the group, and there is a sense in which we *want* to conform. We are part of a social group, and what clothes we wear says something about the group to which we belong. There is a deep human desire to be part of a group. We have a *need* to belong. The question concerns the relationship between social norms and religious convention.

We can see how practices of a social or cultural nature become identified with Christian practice. Some years ago it would not have been socially acceptable to go to church without a hat. Not wearing a hat would indicate a lack of respect for the Lord. Today few people wear hats to church; but is it therefore acceptable or unacceptable for young people to wear baseball caps in church? Is this somehow irreverent? In some places, the same could also be said of wearing shorts or flip-flops. Rebellion against, or lack of conformity to socially acceptable norms, especially by young people, can be viewed as rebellion against God. There is often a tension between what is *culturally* acceptable and what is *religiously* acceptable to your particular group. How these questions are resolved and the interaction between the two will vary from group to group.

Christian believers do not all wear the same clothes, and for many church communities, there is no specific or obvious control. For the most part, Christian identity is no longer expressed overtly in the way we dress. If Christians are to show their distinctiveness today, they probably have to do it in other ways. Over and above social acceptability, in terms of group identity, is there such a thing as Christian clothing? Is it possible to tell if someone is a Christian just by looking at what they are wearing? We will come on to this question in the next chapter.

## Discussion

1.  Can you share details of any occasions when you felt
    awkward because what you were wearing did not match
    the etiquette or dress code?
2.  Is there an expected dress code for what you do every
    day, employed or otherwise?
3.  When you imagine the twelve disciples, what are they
    wearing? All they all wearing the same thing?
4.  Is there an expected dress code at your church? How far
    does or should religious conviction be expressed in what
    is acceptable or allowable for members to wear?
5.  How might Christian identity be expressed, if not
    through distinctive clothes?

Lord, I come to you,
Let my heart be changed, renewed,
Flowing from the grace
That I found in You.
And Lord, I've come to know
The weaknesses I see in me
Will be stripped away
By the power of Your love.

(Geoff Bullock, written 1992)

# 5

## DOES MY FAITH LOOK BIG IN THIS?
### *Christian Clothing?*

'What on earth am I going to wear'? 'I've got nothing to wear'! For some, this type of clothes-related panic sends stress levels soaring. For others, the answer is exciting and planning an outfit is an enjoyable experience. There are certainly some aspects of the fashion industry which exist to play on our insecurities, and we have seen how group and social identities can be very strong influences.

Non-conformity to social expectations can sometimes be viewed as a sign of weakness—in the playground or in the boardroom. If we adorn ourselves appropriately, we can escape teasing and hopefully succeed in life, and be protected from negative judgements by our peers. We do all naturally want to know what is expected at a particular occasion or event, what is considered 'normal'. We want to feel comfortable and fit in.

What you choose to wear at any particular time or at a specific event can be a bit of a minefield to negotiate. Looking too casual can send a message that you don't care; you may not get the job, or you may get left behind. On the other hand, if you are too smart you can be 'over-dressed', which might suggest you spend all your time shopping or in front of the mirror, and care more about your looks than getting the job done.

What you choose to wear can send all sorts of messages, intentional or unintentional, subtle or not so subtle. Amanda Spencer, who was found guilty of arranging the prostitution of five young girls between 2006 and 2011, ordered her victims to wear 'provocative clothes and make-up' before taking them to 'parties'.[1]

On January 24, 2011, Toronto Police Constable Michael Sanguinetti, addressing the issue of campus rape said: "I've been told I'm not supposed to say this—however, women should avoid dressing like sluts in order not to be victimized." He has since apologised for his remarks and has been disciplined by the Toronto police. Later, some 3,000 people took part in the first "SlutWalk" in Toronto aiming to "re-appropriate" the word slut.[2]

Any attack or unwanted approach by a man to a woman is always wrong. But it could also be that women may need to exercise a sense of responsibility in relation to their appearance. There is a fine line between women dressing comfortably and according to their own taste, and where a certain style, deliberately or unconsciously, steps over into something more overtly sexual.

At any particular social occasion, you want to be appropriately dressed so that you will fit in, especially if you are a 'visitor'. We don't want to stand out and look different. In a Presbyterian church in Cambridge in the early 1900s the annual advance of winter was marked by what came to be known as 'moth-ball Sunday', when heavy furs were brought out of storage.[3] What you wear for going to church may be more of a concern for 'outsiders' than 'insiders'.

Does it matter what you wear to church, to come before God or into God's presence? In some communities, perhaps especially African ones, wearing one's best to Sunday services, complete with elaborate hair styles and flamboyant clothing, is very important. This is a cultural norm, but it may have its origins as an expression of hope for a freedom previously unattainable, as well as an exercise in preparation for salvation, here on earth and in the world to come.[4]

In the Jewish tradition, men wrap themselves in a prayer shawl (*tallit*) to promote a proper mood of reverence for God and a prayerful spirit during worship. Tassels or fringes (*tzitzit*) are attached to the corners or edges of the shawl as a reminder to keep God's commandments (Num. 15:37–41).[5]

A vicar was slightly caught out when taking a baptism service immediately after leading a service for students. He was wearing a dog collar, along with a rather casual shirt and jeans, in order to make the church and Christianity acceptable, approachable and non-threatening. The baptism party, on the other hand, had a very strong sense of the occasion, and arrived in the full works, dressed in suits, hats and heels, ready for a big celebration.

What role or status people have can often be identified by looking at what they are wearing. Does it matter what your church leaders are wearing? If an individual is wearing a dog collar, it is a visible sign of the nature of their calling. It is a sign that they have been specifically set apart for this task, and that of itself carries a certain authority.

Should Christian ministers wear dog collars all of the time? Some say yes: such things identify that the minister is different, and not just 'one of us' but someone who has a special role in relation to God. You can be identified as a 'person of God' in the street, and this is part of your role and mission. A minister wearing specially decorated robes speaks of the glory and majesty of God, because they provide a sense of dignity and occasion.

Some say no: dog collars and robes speak of difference from 'ordinary' people and can create barriers and separation between the minister and the people. If ministers wish to identify with the people, they must look and dress like them.[6]

How far do you accommodate who you are and how you dress to the prevailing culture? How and when do you remain different and separate? 'Looks matter', however much we say they don't, most of the time, they do.

If ministers cannot always be identified by what they are wearing, and congregations tend towards some sort of homogeneity, is it possible to tell a group of Christians by what they are wearing? Are there any clothing norms which might apply to Christians in general? The question is framed here in broad terms, not in relation to clothing as an identification with a very specific group, as discussed earlier. Apart from 'Jesus sandals', is there such a thing as Christian clothing? Richard Foster suggests one answer:

Hang the fashions. Buy only what you need. Wear your clothes until they are worn out.[7]

While we may partly agree with the sentiment here, I am not sure that this addresses the real question and also whether it is very practical. As Christians we are not necessarily bound to go round wearing worn out clothes full of holes.

In the second century, the *Epistle to Diognetus* celebrates the fact that Christians are *not* differentiated from others by their clothes or by their food. They follow local customs in what they wear and eat. 'Following the customs of the natives in respect to clothing, food, and the rest of their ordinary conduct, they display to us their wonderful and confessedly striking method of life'.[8]

In general, you probably can't tell a group of Christians just by the way they dress. But there may be some clues, if you look carefully, by also noting what they are *not* wearing. This doesn't mean that there aren't distinguishing features of Christian clothing, or a Christian's attitude towards clothing. This question of believers' attitudes to clothes and ornamentation is not new. Tertullian, writing in the second century, covers similar topics in his advice:

> That salvation—and not (the salvation) of women only, but likewise of men—consists in the exhibition principally of modesty. For since, by the introduction into an appropriation of the Holy Spirit, we are all 'the temple of God'.[9]

For women:

> For they who rub their skin with medicaments, stain their cheeks with rouge, make their eyes prominent with antimony, sin against Him . . . Whatever, then, is plastered on (that) is the devil's work.[10]

For men:

> (such as) to cut the beard too sharply; to pluck it out here and there; to shave round about (the mouth); to arrange the hair, and disguise its hoariness by dyes . . .

to take every opportunity for consulting the mirror; to
gaze anxiously into it . . . all these things are rejected as
frivolous, as hostile to modesty.[11]

So debates about looks and clothes have been going on for a
long time. Three general points may be relevant to us here,
and these relate to fashion, money and modesty.

In relation to fashion, I suggest that it is acceptable for
Christians to be dressed appropriately for the occasion.
Church-goers should not have to be labelled as frumpy,
or wear the most boring clothes possible. Clothes fashions
change, clothes wear out and need replacing and there is a
need to dress appropriately for whatever we are doing. On
the other hand, there is no need to follow every whim, twist
and turn of the fashion industry. If, as a Christian, you are
aware that your ultimate and true identity is elsewhere, that
is, in Christ, then fashion of itself becomes less important.

Simon Ward, former Chief Operating Officer of the
British Fashion Council, says:

Inner character is where you start and invest most.
Fashion can help us then express our identity and character. We need to move away from image, which is
about dressing to impress, and think instead of dressing
to express.[12]

This approach may be viewed as a contrast between the inner and outer self (see also Rom. 7:22; 2 Cor. 4:16; Eph.
3:16):

Your beauty should not come from outward adornment,
such as braided hair and the wearing of gold jewellery

and fine clothes. Instead, it should be that of our inner
self, the unfading beauty of a gentle and quiet spirit,
which is of great worth in God's sight.

1 Peter 3:3, 4[13]

Peter has also said earlier that the 'genuineness of your
faith' is more precious than gold, which is perishing (1:7).
This encourages his readers to focus on the inner self, which
should grow more beautiful, unlike the outer self which
fades. God is very aware of the orientation of our hearts,
and is not swayed by outward appearance (see the choice of
David in 1 Sam. 16:7).

Concerning money, many Christians give very generous-
ly to churches, ministries and charities, and are not wasteful
of their God-given resources. Some may choose to support local charity shops or agencies by buying clothes there,
both for financial as well as ethical reasons. Why buy cheap
T-shirts, laboured over in the developing world for less than
a living wage, when you could extend the life of other types
of garments by up-cycling? The amount of money chosen or
allocated to spend on clothes may therefore be less within
the Christian community than elsewhere.

Lastly, in relation to modesty: while what is considered
acceptable modesty will vary between cultures, this can be
an issue, especially for Christian girls in western society.
The wearing of skimpy tops and skirts which reveal significant amounts of your body, is probably something believers
would avoid. Such dress invites explicit sexual advance and
reflects an approach to sexuality at odds with mainstream
Christian teaching.

This is not something new either. In his novel, *The History*

*of Tom Jones,* written in 1749, one of Henry Fielding's ladies'
comments:

> I saw two farmers' daughters at church, the other day, with
> bare necks. I protest they shocked me. If wenches will hang
> out lures for fellows, it is no matter what they suffer.[14]

In a consumerist culture, we are hard-pressed not to be concerned about our appearance. But knowing Christ can give
an inner confidence; Christians are not primarily defined
by what is on the outside. That is not the same as saying, 'I
don't care what I wear', but rather knowing that it is not of
ultimate significance.

Matthew tends to be thought of as a rather austere gospel,
but in chapter 6 he records some of Jesus' most comforting
words. Living as a believer in this world is not an easy task,
but there is no need to fret and worry, because the heavenly Father takes care of his children.[15] Just as you cannot
serve God and wealth (mammon, 6:24), you cannot be sustained by both faith and anxiety; so, repeated five times is
the phrase, 'do not worry' (6:25, 27, 28, 31, 34).

> Therefore I tell you, do not worry about your life, what
> you will eat or what you will drink, or about your body,
> what you will wear. Is not life more than food, and the
> body more than clothing? . . . And why do you worry
> about clothing? Consider the lilies of the field, how
> they grow; they neither toil nor spin, yet I tell you, even
> Solomon in all his glory was not clothed like one of these.
>
>                                        Matt. 6:25, 28, 29[16]

Instead of looking at the fashions, walk out into the
fields and look at the wild flowers. They never primp

or shop, but have you ever seen colour and design quite like it? The ten best-dressed men and women in the country look shabby alongside them.

*The Message*

However much we know this in our heads, intellectually, and in spite of culture and the fashion industry's best attempts, we have to keep reminding ourselves that dress and clothing is not a way to achieve perfection or happiness. It is also probably true that the opposite path of extreme forms of aestheticism in relation to clothing and bodies do not achieve happiness either.

This leads on to thinking a little more about how we understand our relationship with our bodies. Sometimes we can assume that the better way is to put mind over matter; reason over emotion; soul over body. Yet if we assume that God loves everything he has made, and that he has given us bodies, then that body is something he loves, something to be cherished and cared for, rather than ignored, endured or abused. We note that Jesus says, 'You cannot make one hair white or black' and that you cannot 'add one cubit to your height or a single hour to your span of life' by worrying (Matt. 5:36; 6:27).

Anything related to our physical natures is not necessarily less important than our rational or spiritual endeavours. This respect for the body is shown decisively in the incarnation—Christ 'put on' human flesh. The incarnation becomes almost like a form of dress, although of course it is much more than that.

Since the children are made of flesh and blood, it's logical that the Saviour took on flesh and blood in order to rescue them by his death.

Heb. 2:14; *The Message*; cf. John 1:14

This means that God understands the ambiguities and mess-iness of embodied existence. We are created in the image of God *and* we are finite. 'An incarnational attitude makes peace with one's imperfect body that neither a good outfit nor a face-lift can make immortal'.[17]

One of the reasons we need to look after our bodies now is that we will retain our bodies in some form after death. We do not *have* a body which will be discarded, but we *are* a body which will be retained in some form. Paul writes about this subject in 2 Cor. 4:16—5:5.[18] This is a complex passage in which he uses a whole series of metaphors and pictures, seemingly struggling to find the right one. He compares our present bodies to a tent, a temporary dwelling place or tab-ernacle for God's Spirit; this will be replaced by a permanent dwelling, like a temple.

Paul then switches from talking about tents to clothing. 'Clothing' here appears to refer to bodies, either the bodies we have at the moment or our resurrection bodies. He doesn't want to be 'unclothed', ie without a body, but rather longs to be 'further clothed' with a new body which will be permanent; not disembodied, but re-embodied; definitely not naked without any clothing; not unclothed, but more fully clothed (see also 1 Cor. 15:52, 54). The word Paul uses here for 'enclothed' has the meaning 'to get more dressed' or 'to put extra' clothing on over the top. This implies that what is already there, underneath, is of vital importance, and cannot be done away with or left behind.

Tom Wright suggests that:

(Paul) had come to realize that the present body is only the beginning, the initial clothing for a true self that will one day be much more fully clothed. That is total-ly different from saying 'the present body is the outer shell for a true self which is non-bodily and will one day, thank God, be freed from the whole business of bodies'.[19]

If an incarnational attitude may be helpful for us in terms of making peace with our own bodies, do any of the same principles or attitudes apply to the wider body of Christ, the church? Just as you need to make peace with your own physical body, with its joys and frustrations, flaws and beau-ty, is there a similar way in which we need, could or should make peace with the corporate body of the church? We are a body individually and also a body corporately as the 'body of Christ'.

On the one hand, in our mobile and consumer oriented society, we can try a church for size, to see if it fits: does it meet our needs and expectations? If it doesn't, in this 'must-fit-me-precisely' culture, we can move on.[20] We no longer 'put on' religion or church, but we can 'try it on' for size, taste and preference—believing without belonging. We all have preferences and engage with God in different ways. On the other hand, 'A spirituality that has no institution-al structure or support very soon becomes self-indulgent and subjective and one-generational'.[21] Such a spirituality also becomes very vulnerable to reduction to an individual lowest common religious denominator. It would also be im-portant that the gospel that is being proclaimed is the word of the cross and not some form of human 'boasting' through image manipulation.

As we have seen earlier, the change in status in becoming a believer and being baptised, is something both individual and communal—and as a member of the church you are forced to relate to others of a similar status, but not necessarily of similar outlook and opinion. Becoming a baptised member of this community isn't just a practical matter; it isn't just so that we can all get along and be nice to each other. 'It is rather that something essential to being Messiah-people is lost when the community is split'.[22] A fundamental aspect of being in fellowship in Jesus is lost if the community is fragmented.

As individuals, what we would actually like to do most of the time is relate to those who are similar to ourselves. This is easy and comfortable; we are all wearing the same type of clothes. Corporately, we find a deep bond of fellowship in Christ. What Jesus calls us to do is also to relate to those who are different from ourselves; those who are wearing something completely different.

So, can you tell a Christian, or a group of Christians, just by the way they dress? Probably not. Would it be helpful, convenient or useful if you could? Again, probably not. In our culture, which is very dependent on the impact of the visual, of image and of fashion, Christians are not immune from its influence, but neither are they bound by it. We are witnesses to something we have not seen as such and cannot visibly show others, except by our own conviction and behaviour.

## Discussion

1.  'I cannot make up my mind whether high heels are a
    liberating personal choice or a sign of cultural enslave-
    ment' (Angela Tilby, *Church Times*, 3:06:16). What do
    you think?
2.  Think about ways in which we love, honour, respect and
    cherish our bodies; and then consider the ways in which
    bodies can be glamorised, trivialised and exploited.
3.  The Christian faith imposes no universal rules in
    relation to clothing or food. Food should be eaten 'in
    thanksgiving to God'. Do you think that something
    similar applies to the wearing of clothes?
4.  Should you be able to tell if someone is a Christian by
    what they are wearing? Should aiming to be a good
    witness to your faith affect what you wear?
5.  How far do you think the Holy Spirit influences what
    you wear?

When He shall come with trumpet sound,
Oh, may I then in Him be found;
Dressed in His righteousness alone,
Faultless stand before the throne.
On Christ the solid rock I stand
All other ground is sinking sand.

                    *The Solid Rock*, Edward Mote (1797–1874)

# 6

# 'AND THEY GAMBLED FOR HIS CLOTHES'
*The Passion Narratives*

There are relatively few references to clothing in the gospel stories, but when reading the passion narratives looking out for mentions of clothing, quite a significant number stand out. This is particularly the case in John's gospel, but there are references to clothing in Mark, Matthew and Luke as well. When reading the passion narrative, I would not normally advocate switching from one gospel to another, as by doing this I think the overall dynamic and themes of an individual gospel can easily be lost. Yet when looking at this particular theme of clothing, a reading which combines elements from all four passion narratives is more appropriate. We begin in Mark's gospel.

### Bartimaeus: Mark 10:46–52
A story involving clothing functions as a bridge between the second and third sections of Mark's gospel. Bartimaeus casting off his cloak comes at the end of the central teaching section (8:22—10:52)[1] but also provides a link to the beginning of Mark's passion narrative.

Bartimaeus is named here, which is unusual for a gospel story. He is a 'blind beggar', lacking physical sight and means, and he is 'sitting by the roadside', thus excluded from the group of both the disciples and the crowd. When he hears Jesus is going by, he shouts, 'Son of David, have mercy on me'; this is the only time this phrase is used in Mark's gospel and is the first, public and unrebuked recognition of Jesus in Mark.

When Jesus 'stood still' and called him, there is a dramatic pause in the action, and a stopping on his journey. Bartimaeus 'threw off his cloak', 'sprang up' and 'came to' Jesus, in direct contrast with his previous 'sitting'. Jesus heals him and then he 'followed' Jesus 'on the way',[2] the way to Jerusalem and the way of suffering.

The three incidents immediately before this story in Mark form an instructive contrast. To the rich young man, Jesus says, 'Sell what you own . . . come, follow me' (10:21). This he is unable to do, contrasting Bartimaeus' throwing off his cloak and following. For the disciples, Peter takes this a stage further and says, 'Look, we *have* left everything and followed you' (v. 28), but even this kind of commitment does not bring with it the right to be 'first' (v. 31).

James and John also address Jesus as 'Teacher', but ask Jesus, 'We want you to do for us whatever we ask of you' (10:35). Jesus replies, 'What is it you want me to do for you'?, the same words he says to Bartimaeus (v. 51). Jesus cannot grant their request, because they are asking for positions of power and have misunderstood the nature of the Kingdom and of Jesus' role (10:43–45).

Bartimaeus, on the other hand, and in sharp contrast, throws off his cloak, asks for mercy and then follows. What we see in Bartimaeus is a model response to Jesus. His cloak symbolises various things: it may be the item he spread out to collect alms; it may have been his only possession; the only thing that kept him a trace warm at night. By throwing it off, he is truly abandoning everything to go to Jesus. This is a genuine act of faith, because, if you are blind, and throw off your cloak, you have little chance of finding it again. He really was leaving everything behind.

Symbolically, we need to come to Jesus in obedience to be given insight, and it is Jesus who can heal spiritual blindness. There is a contrast with the disciples and the crowd, who have physical sight but are blind, and Bartimaeus, who is blind but has spiritual sight/insight. Leaving everything behind to follow Jesus calls for a radical break with the past. Throwing off his cloak suggests a seizing of the moment to come to Jesus in response to his call. Bartimaeus already knew who Jesus was, so the story further suggests that following is something continuous, and may be punctuated by such significant moments when a specific response is required.[3]

### Jesus' entry into Jerusalem: Mark 11:1–11

The language of cloaks and Son of David is carried forward into the next incident which describes Jesus' entry into the city.[4] Two disciples, on bringing the colt to Jesus, 'threw their cloaks on it'. This most naturally refers to the outer coats of the disciples who use them to form a saddle cloth. This may sound like quite a normal thing to do, but when 'many people spread their cloaks on the road', there is clearly more going on here.

As with Sir Walter Raleigh putting his cloak on the ground so that Queen Elizabeth could walk over it without getting her feet muddy, the gesture implies that you are recognising

the other person's status and authority. We see this indication of submission to the newly anointed king Jehu, when
his supporters spread their cloaks under his feet on the bare
steps as a sign of loyalty (2 Kings 9:13).

Solomon rode on David's mule to be anointed king (1
Kings 1:33), and Matthew (21:7, 8) who records the event
as a popular triumph in contrast to Mark and Luke where
the messianic aspect is more restrained, sees the incident
as a fulfilment of prophecy (Zech. 9:9). The crowds shout,
'Hosanna to the Son of David'!, which, along with the riding
rather than walking, and the cloaks on the road, point towards a royal event.

In terms of the gospel story, this is not just the entry into
Jerusalem, but it is also the entry into the remainder of
the narrative. Jesus leaves the sympathetic pilgrim crowds
outside, on the way in, to then encounter the hostility of
the city.

## Foot washing: John 13:1–20

We now move to an event recorded in John's gospel, Jesus
washing the disciples' feet (13:1–20). John's extended passion narrative begins with an action which is not part of
Passover, but a normal feature of hospitality (Luke 7:44).
The foot-washing should have been done on the arrival of
the guests, not after the meal had begun. It should also have
been done by the lowest slave, not by a guest or Jesus himself. Both these different features suggest that things are not
as they seem.

A significant key is given at the beginning of the chapter
when we read that 'Jesus knew that his hour had come', that
is, the hour of the event of his death and going to his Father

(13:1). Earlier in the gospel and up to a significant turning point in 12:20, Jesus' 'hour' has not yet come (2:4; 7:30; 8:20). But when some Greeks arrive and want to see him, Jesus answers, 'The hour has come for the Son of Man to be glorified'. This is the first time in the gospel that Jesus' message has gone out to the Gentiles, in the form of the Greeks, and away from those John describes as 'the Jews'.

So this is the context in which Jesus 'rose from supper, laid aside his garments',[5] suggesting that something special is also going on here. The word John chooses for 'laid aside'[6] is the same word he has used earlier in chapter 10. There he shows how the shepherd loves his sheep, and the greatest thing the shepherd can do for them is to lay aside or lay down his life for them (10:11, 15, 17).

John's literary style is frequently to use synonyms, rather than remaining with the same word. The fact that he has chosen to use the same word is significant, especially as the word in question is not that usually used for the laying aside of garments,[7] but for being laid in the tomb or laying down one's life. The word is used again very shortly afterwards in 13:37–8 to refer exactly to this. This is the humility of the cross as acted out by Jesus before the event.

The inclusion of Judas in the foot washing troubles us. According to John, Jesus knows that Judas, one of the disciples he has chosen, is a devil and a thief (6:70; 12:4–5). Jesus washes all the disciples' feet, but Judas remains unclean (13:10–11). The washing may somehow be symbolic of Jesus laying aside his life on the cross as a way of embracing, knowing and overcoming the darkness found in Judas, and in us.

We need a particular kind of receptivity to have our feet washed; taking our shoes and socks off at a Maundy

Thursday foot-washing service, can be a very humbling experience. It is difficult to stand on your dignity in bare feet, and receive service and washing, and maybe also a kiss, from someone else. Washing the whole body suggests *complete* submission to the end; and we can only do this if we accept that Jesus has in fact 'laid aside' everything for us.

For John, the Word became flesh in order to wash our feet. The next time Jesus has his clothes changed, he is being mocked as a king (19:5).

## Arrest: Mark 14:51–2

We come now to Jesus' arrest and to an incident recorded only in Mark's gospel. This concerns a young man who was following Jesus 'wearing nothing but a linen cloth'. When he too was seized, he 'left the linen cloth and ran off naked'.

The significance of this incident is hard to determine, and perhaps the other gospel writers felt this too, as they have not included it in their accounts. Parallels have been suggested to Adam and Eve hiding their nakedness in a garden; or perhaps to Joseph who escapes from Pharaoh's wife by leaving his garment behind (Gen. 39:12). Others have suggested connections with the 'young man' at the tomb (Mark 16:5); or perhaps this young man was Mark himself. There seems to be no clear answer.[8]

Yet the inclusion of this incident does provide a direct contrast to the description of Bartimaeus; both leave their garments behind, but one does everything right, and the other everything wrong. Bartimaeus recognises and calls on Jesus; he gives up everything he owns and his means of livelihood, his warmth and covering; he comes to Jesus and then follows him on the way.

The other young man, while initially following, runs away; he suffers what seems to be a shameful nudity in cowardly flight; he leaves behind both his garment as well as Jesus. His action emphasises the increasing isolation of Jesus in his passion, and his actions highlight the fact that 'all of them deserted him and fled' (14:50).

### Caiaphas tears his robes: Matthew 26:65

Jesus is arrested and tried before Caiaphas, the high priest, and the Sanhedrin. Caiaphas questions Jesus, and asks, not, 'Who are you'?, but, 'tell us if you are the Messiah, the Son of God'?, hence posing a question in terms that ironically reveal the answer (cf. 26:25 and 27:11; 16:16). Caiaphas' questioning of Jesus is not a genuine search for the truth of the matter, but rather is a pretext for a previously stated purpose, that of killing him (26:4). On hearing Jesus' words of reply, he tears his clothes and declares the answer Jesus has given under oath to be blasphemy, whether or not this was legally the case.[9] Other members of the Sanhedrin would be unlikely to disagree.

Clothes were torn deliberately as a sign of sorrow, anger, mourning, or on hearing blasphemy. Jacob tears his clothes on hearing of the death of Joseph (Gen. 37:34), and David does the same on hearing of the deaths of Saul and Jonathan (2 Sam. 1:11–12).[10] The prophet Joel encourages his hearers to return to the Lord: 'Rend your heart and not your clothing' (2:12).

In Matthew, there is something else going on with this 'tearing' too. Mark (14:63) records the high priest tearing his 'tunic' (*chiton*), whereas Matthew uses a slightly different word, his 'garment' or cloak (*himatia*). Matthew's choice of

word follows that of the Greek found in Lev. 21:10, where
a priest is forbidden to tear his robes. Given the elaborate instructions for the priests' robes in Exodus (28), this
is hardly surprising.[11] Nonetheless, the change in wording
may be significant, as it brings the high priest's action into
line with Matthew's heightened criticism of the Jewish leaders. Although they appear to be concerned with keeping the
law, there are many points in the episode at which this is
suspect. They are seeking false witnesses (forbidden in Ex.
20:16; Deut. 5:20); the tearing of robes is forbidden; and
the trial takes place at night.[12] In saying that Jesus, who has
spoken the truth, has blasphemed, they themselves are ironically guilty of blasphemy.

Another 'tearing' takes place at the time of Jesus' death.
'The curtain of the temple was torn in two, from top to
bottom' (27:51). Jesus had earlier predicted the destruction
of the temple (24:2), and so this tearing of the curtain, not
only suggests the opening of a new way of access to God,
but also that the temple will no longer be there.[13]

In an age when any kind of garment must have been precious to its owner, for someone to tear a garment seems like
a pretty drastic step. Could they then be mended? Were they
torn down a seam, or perhaps they had a ritual special place
in which an opening was loosely stitched together and, as it
were, became available for tearing, a bit like today's velcro?

Later Jewish writings tell of judges who, as a symbolic,
ritual act, tear their clothes in response to hearing blasphemy: 'the judges rise up and tear their garments so that they
can never be mended' (or this can be translated: ' they may
not mend them again') (*M.Sanh* 7:5) This seems to suggest
that, under some circumstances, they could in fact have

been mended.

In Jewish tradition today, part of the funeral ritual is a moment during which members of the immediate family rend or tear their garments as a symbol of their grief. This can also be done by the rabbi who will cut a specially positioned piece of black ribbon on the mourners' clothes.

Today, some may tear their clothes deliberately as a fashion statement, but generally torn clothes indicate someone is poor or has had an accident. 'Tearing' language can also be used symbolically, as in 'tearing your hair out', not literally, but to indicate extreme frustration when things aren't going right (often with technology).

### Soldiers mock Jesus as king—the purple robe: John 19:1–5

In the first part of the gospel narratives, Jesus is the active one—travelling, teaching, healing, bringing the Kingdom of God. Once he is 'handed over' his role becomes more passive; he becomes the one who is 'done to' by others. There is a series of 'handing overs'—by Judas to the priests; by the priests to Pilate; by Pilate to the crowd, and in Luke by Pilate to Herod and back.[14]

Pilate's Roman soldiers mock Jesus as King of the Jews with a crown of thorns and a purple cloak (Mark 15:17; John 19:2) or a scarlet robe (Matt. 27:28). Mark says that the cloak was purple. Purple dye was made from Mediterranean molluscs, which meant it was very expensive and so the colour was associated with wealth and royalty. Scarlet dye came from insects and was cheaper. It was also the colour of Roman soldiers' cloaks. So Matthew may be recording that the soldiers used readily available objects (a soldier's cloak, thorn twigs and cane) to parody royal regalia (robe, crown and sceptre). Scenes of mockery were well known at the time, at actual events mocking lunatics or prisoners, as well as in games, at the theatre or at festivals.[15]

John (19:4) records that Pilate brings out Jesus already dressed up as a laughing-stock. This is inviting a hostile response, the opposite of the conditions required for a considered judgement of the case. The motive 'to let you know that I find no case against him' (repeated three times: 18:38; 19:4, 6), is a lame excuse. Jesus is dressed as a king, but is announced as a man; 'Here is the man'! (19:5).

Roman soldiers, acting evidently not on an order but on their own, are making fun of Jesus for their own amusement. But the truth is that this seemingly passive person, the one dressed up in a purple robe and mocked, is indeed a king. Things are the opposite of what they seem to be. The judge of the world stands before a lesser judge. The governor does not govern. The crowds prefer to free a criminal instead of an innocent man. Pilate does not take responsibility when he should be in charge. Jesus rules from a cross and not a throne. He is not served but serves and gives his life for others.

## The legend of Veronica

Matthew, Mark and Luke (27:32; 15;21; 23:26) refer to Simon of Cyrene being compelled to carry Jesus' cross, whereas John 19:17 refers to Jesus carrying his own cross. Legend tells of a woman of Jerusalem who wiped Jesus' face with a veil while he was on the way to Calvary. According to tradition, and represented in the traditional Stations of the Cross, the cloth was imprinted with the image of Jesus' face. Much later, the woman was identified with the woman who suffered from an issue of blood, who touched Jesus' cloak and was healed (Mark 5:27; Matt. 9:21; Luke 8:44).

**Jesus is naked**

After the mocking, the soldiers 'stripped him of the purple cloak and put his own clothes on him' (Mark 15:20). Later they took his clothes again after the crucifixion to divide them up amongst themselves. Specific details of the nature of crucifixion are not mentioned in the gospel accounts, possibly because they were well known. The text baldly says, 'And they crucified him' (Mark 15:24). The victim is unarmed, weak, unprotected, vulnerable and completely shamed by being stripped naked. We have seen how nakedness is not only a total humiliation, but also a warning to others, a manifestation of what a stronger power in authority can do to a weaker one, or to those who disobey, or don't fit in.

**Jesus' tunic—gambling for his clothes: John 19:23, 24**

It was customary for soldiers on duty to share out the personal belongings, including clothes, of an executed man. This fact is mentioned in all of the gospels, but John draws out and develops more of the significance (Matt. 27:35; Mark 15:24; Luke 23:34; John 19:23, 24).

There are more explicit references to scripture in John, suggesting that John was concerned to spell out the way in which everything that happened took place in accordance with the scriptures.[16] In relation to Jesus' clothes, he refers to Psalm 22:18:

> They divided my clothes among themselves,
> And for my clothing they cast lots.[17]

In discussing this psalm, Jonathan Magonet notes:

> The Psalm seems to have had an important place in the popular consciousness, which is borne out by the fact that there is also a well-developed Rabbinic tradition, to be found in the Midrash on Psalms, of reading the Psalm as a reflection of the experience of Queen Esther.[18]

Esther is about to go to the king to plead for her people, which she knows 'is not according to the law'.

> The people of the palace began to say: 'Now the king will be angry at Esther, and death will be decreed for her'. And every one said: 'I shall take Esther's apparel', this one saying 'Me I shall take her ornaments'; and that one saying 'Me, I shall take her earrings'.[19]

John records that the soldiers divided Jesus' clothes into four parts. It is doubtful whether Jesus would have had four pieces of clothing to be divided; or perhaps what he had was too poor to be worth keeping, so they tore them up; or perhaps this is John's way of emphasising that there were four soldiers—a band of four needed to keep a naked man in his place.

John goes on to make a distinction between the clothes, which were merely divided, and the tunic, for which lots were cast. The tunic (*chiton*), the garment worn next to the skin is described as 'seamless, woven in one piece from top to bottom'. So this was not just any old under garment, but has significance.

There have been two main understandings of what this might mean. Some see specific priestly parallels. Aaron is instructed to wear 'holy vestments' including the 'holy linen tunic' (Lev. 16:4; 21:10). Josephus tells us that the long outer robe of blue of the High Priest was woven without seams, and had a vertical slit for the head and slits at the sides for the arms.[20] Jesus has been portrayed as a king by the title on the cross. Here this tunic means he is also portrayed as a priest, indicated earlier by what is generally known as Jesus' High-Priestly Prayer, in chapters 14–17.

Another understanding of the tunic has to do with unity. The fact that the tunic is without a seam and was not torn has been seen as symbolising unity among Jesus' followers in the new era /kingdom which Jesus brings. This is in contrast to the incident recorded in I Kings 11:30–1, where the opposite is portrayed, and the prophet Ahijah tears his new robe (*himation*) into 12 pieces to symbolise the rending of the kingdom.

There are often quite complex layers of meaning in John's Gospel, and the specific significance of the seamless tunic can be interpreted differently.[21] By way of contrast, the guards appear to be at ease, clothed, sitting and gambling, maybe drinking, while someone else dies, naked.

### Grave clothes

Joseph of Arimathea, described as a disciple of Jesus, has Pilate's permission to take away Jesus' body. All four gospels record that he wrapped the body in a linen shroud or cloth, as well as indicating that this has to be done quickly before the start of the Sabbath.[22]

The body was laid on a length of cloth, long enough to come back over the head and down to the feet. Bandages or strips were then wrapped round in order to keep the limbs in position. A face cloth was tied under the chin to keep the jaw in place. It is this cloth John may be referring to as the 'cloth which had been on Jesus' head' (John 20:7). There is a similar reference in the story of Lazarus, who 'came out, his hands and feet bound with strips of cloth, and his face wrapped in a cloth' (John 11:44).

The English word 'wrapped' might suggest to us a link with Luke's account of Jesus' birth, where Mary 'wrapped him in swaddling cloths'. Although the Greek words for 'wrapped' and 'swaddled' are different, both serve a similar purpose: for a new born and a dead body, the aim is to keep the limbs in position, and enfold a naked body. By wrapping his body in a linen shroud something honourable has been done to Jesus' body, which is in sharp contrast to all the dishonourable acts done to his body in Jerusalem.

In John's account at the tomb, the 'other disciple' (Beloved Disciple) reaches the tomb first, and 'saw the linen wrappings lying there'. Simon Peter arrives, goes in, and he too 'saw the linen wrappings lying there, and the cloth that had been on Jesus' head, not lying with the linen wrappings but rolled up in a place by itself' (John 20:5–7).

The linen cloths (in Greek the *lying sheets*) are mentioned three times (vv. 5, 6 and 7), and the words imply that they are just 'lying there', limp, 'like a collapsed balloon when the air has gone out of it'.[23] Alison Still, describes her sculpture of hanging cloth like 'a garment emptied of its human wearer'; sadness, limp, empty; an empty tomb indicating an absence of presence.[24]

All three references suggest that John wants to emphasise that the grave cloths were undisturbed by the resurrection. This is not the work of either Jesus tidying up after himself, or of angels folding the grave clothes (as in the hymn *Thine be the glory*) or of tomb robbers working quickly and leaving a mess. This is something different and deliberate. Jesus had apparently passed through them.

The actual significance of the head cloth being rolled or wrapped up 'in a place by itself' (not folded) is hard to determine. But the word used for 'wrapped up' here is the same as that used in Matthew (27:59) and Luke (23:53) where Joseph of Arimethea wrapped the body with grave cloths, again suggesting that the wrappings on Jesus' head, while they may have been separate, were also undisturbed.

The question has been asked as to whether someone provided Jesus with resurrection clothes?[25] Where did he get them from? It has been suggested that Jesus had already left a bag of clothes in the garden earlier, or that he found some in the gardener's shed (John 20:15), or that he found the linen cloth belonging to the young man who fled naked. These explanations seem to be both too fanciful and too literal, trying to answer an unanswerable and probably irrelevant question.

There is a complete lack of description of the physical appearance of the risen Jesus, and of what he is wearing. The risen Jesus just appears (Matt. 28:9, 17; John 21:7); Mary does not recognise him until he speaks (John 20:16); he is made known to two other disciples at Emmaus in the breaking of bread (Luke 24:31); and to Thomas by the invitation to touch (John 20:27).

By way of contrast, when the women arrive at the tomb, they see a man (or men) or angels there, and all four gospels specifically refer to what they are wearing: dazzling white robes.[26] This difference could be because Jesus has existed on earth with a physical body which continues to be recognisable in some way as a resurrection body. This is a different form of existence to that of angelic beings who do not have this unique experience of a physical body.

In the gospel narratives, there are very few references to Jesus' clothing, most of which occur in the Passion Narratives. The other mentions concern the woman with the haemorrhage who touched his garment (Mark 5:27), and at the transfiguration. Here 'his clothes became dazzling white, such as no one on earth could bleach them' (Mark 9:3). If the transfiguration is seen as a proleptic event of Jesus in his glory (that is, one signifying in the present something from the future), this raises the question as to why, in his resurrection appearances, was Jesus not seen like this, in garments of glory?[27]

Perhaps this lack of reference to clothes of glory in the resurrection appearances is to do with the fact that Jesus has not yet ascended to the Father. Luke describes how a 'cloud took him out of their sight'. But then, as the disciples were 'gazing up towards heaven, suddenly two men in white robes stood by them' to tell them that Jesus has been taken into heaven (Acts 1:9–12).

### Peter in the boat and on the shore: John 21

The passion narratives in our four gospels, while varying in some details, record the events of Jesus' death with remarkable consistency. But after the resurrection, the accounts vary considerably. It is as if Jesus has broken the bonds of his earthly existence and appears all over the place.

In John's gospel, Jesus has appeared to Mary, the disciples without Thomas, the disciples with Thomas. Then John records that 'After these things Jesus showed himself again to the disciples' (21:1). Peter and other disciples have decided to go fishing. When the Beloved Disciple tells Peter that the man on the shore is Jesus, Peter 'put on some clothes, for he was naked, and jumped into the lake' (21:7); literally 'wrapped his outer garment around him'.

At one level, Peter did not want to greet Jesus naked;[28] at another level, other symbolism and meaning is probably in mind. As we have come to expect from John, this act of wrapping is significant. It is the same word that Jesus used when wrapping a towel round his waist at the foot washing (13:4). Peter is doing here what Jesus had done earlier. Similar parallels can be found at other points in the story.

Throughout the Passion narrative, we have seen how Jesus becomes more passive, and things are done to him. Jesus now says the same thing about Peter:

> 'Very truly, I tell you, when you were younger you used to fasten your own belt a go wherever you wished. But when you grow old, you will stretch out your hands and someone else will fasten a belt around you and take you where you do not wish to go'. (He said this to indicate the kind of death by which he would glorify God.)'
>
> John 21:18, 19

There is a series of contrasts here: between deciding a course of action for himself (going fishing), and someone else taking him where he doesn't want to go; between throwing a garment round himself, and someone else dressing him; between throwing himself into the lake, and someone else pinning him down.

The words further suggest that in feeding Jesus' sheep, Peter will himself suffer, be crucified, but then, significantly 'glorify God'. Up to this point in the gospel this phrase has been reserved for reference to Jesus himself—he is the one who glorifies God. By wrapping a garment round himself, Peter is doing what Jesus does. 'As the Father has sent me, so I send you' (20:21).

We have looked at how various different aspects of clothing play an important part in the passion narratives. Blind Bartimaeus 'saw' who Jesus was. Throughout the passion narratives many do not 'see' at all, and others 'see' partially. Like the Emperor's new clothes, it takes courage to see and declare what is actually going on. The naked man on the cross does not *look* like royalty. On the cross, he became poor that we might become rich (2 Cor. 8:9), and to that we might add that he became naked that we might be clothed.

## Discussion

1.  Have you ever been forced to wear clothing you didn't want to?
2.  If you have experienced a very difficult situation when you felt stripped of nearly everything, what was left and what kept you going?
3.  Bartimaeus showed a joyous, extravagant and reckless response. The woman of Samaria may have forgotten her water-jar as she ran (John 4:28). This can happen when somehow we become suddenly responsive to the call of Jesus. How does this relate to your experience?
4.  If we are called to come out of the tomb we have wrapped ourselves in, we need to take off all layers of falsity, in order to be ready to be re-clothed. What kinds of unhelpful clothes or cloths do we like to wrap around ourselves?
5.  Following Jesus doesn't get us where we want to go; it gets us to where Jesus is going. How easy is it to recognise the possibility that he will clothe us in garments of his choice, not ours?

Thine be the glory, risen, conquering Son,
Endless is the victory, Thou o'er death hast won;
Angels in bright raiment rolled the stone away,
Kept the folded grave-clothes, where Thy body lay.

Thine be the glory, risen, conquering Son,
Endless is the victory, Thou o'er death hast won.

Tr. Richard B. Hoyle (1854–1932)

# 7

## OVER ALL, PUT ON LOVE
### *Conclusion*

World views can encompass different combinations of religious as well as cultural markers: art, architecture, language, calendar customs and appearance, as well as political and economic ideologies. In this study of clothing as used in biblical language and image, we have looked at how clothing can be a potent symbol of our status—from social, cultural and religious perspectives. Changes in that status are often recognised by a change of clothing.

We have also explored how 'putting on Christ' functions in relation to influencing or controlling our behaviour. Nakedness was found to be significant in describing our relationship with God, and kinship about how that relationship is expressed with others. We have also seen how status, ethics and kinship interact with each other at several different levels.

One well known piece of biblical clothing yet to be mentioned is Joseph's amazing coat, described in Gen. 37:3 as a 'long robe with sleeves'.[1] This is a gift from his father Jacob and identifies Joseph as his favourite. When Joseph's brothers betray him, they strip him, take his garment and stain it with blood, thus convincing Jacob of Joseph's death. Joseph has lost not only his robe, but also his status and freedom.

When Joseph became part of Potiphar's household in Egypt, he may well have worn a garment signifying his status as a slave overseer (39:5). It is this garment which Potiphar's wife pulls off, causing Joseph to lose his status and freedom once again. Later, Pharaoh sends for Joseph to interpret his dreams. Joseph quickly 'shaved and changed his clothes' (41:14), the beginning of his restoration. Later Pharaoh arrayed Joseph in fine linens, gave him a signet ring, and placed a gold chain around his neck in gratitude for his wise interpretation of his dreams (41:42). Joseph later gives provisions and new clothes to his family, as a sign of affection and forgiveness (45:22).

We can see how a series of incidents in the Joseph story involving clothing signal changes of role and status. We have also seen how the passion narratives are punctuated by references to clothing. In a similar way the whole of the biblical narrative about human beings in relation to God can be symbolised by clothing.

The creation narrative shows a perfect relation with God, in a garden and not involving clothing. After that relationship was broken, clothing became necessary as part of human's earthly nature. A time was looked forward to when God would again clothe his people, removing their sin, shame and nakedness. This was achieved by Jesus, naked and shamed on the cross. His death enabled 'the saints' to be fully clothed. The biblical narrative contains images of a re-creation at the end of time. These include both a garden and Sabbath rest,[2] but not obvious references to a return to a state of unselfconscious nakedness.

Rather, the image of the saints described in Revelation

indicates that they are to be clothed in pure white linen robes like those of the angels (Rev. 15:6; 6:11; 19:8). Being clothed in white is a potent symbol of righteousness and purity. The clothing of God himself is described as 'white as snow' (Dan 7:9); Jesus is transfigured in clothes 'dazzling white' (Matt. 17:2); the angels at the empty tomb are similarly in 'dazzling clothes' (Luke 24:5).

The coming of Jesus and the Kingdom of God brings both a new time and a new status for believers. For believers, the dying and rising with Christ in baptism, effects a complete change of status; an old and a new order of existence. The 'old man' corporate identity with Adam has been severed (Rom 6:6) and we have become attached to the 'new man' (Col. 3:10–11; Eph. 2:16; Gal. 3:27). Paul, in writing about the cross, consistently describes Jesus' death as *for us*.[3] Jesus became and achieved something for our benefit. He became sin, a curse, death, under the law, poor, *so that* we might become righteous, a blessing, have life, be free from the law and rich. To this list we might also add that he became naked so that we might become fully clothed.[4] For those who are ready when the master comes, 'he will fasten his belt and have them sit down to eat, and he will come and serve them' (Luke 12:37).

God is creative, and we are made in his image. This means we are creative beings too. There is nothing intrinsically wrong with taking pride and pleasure in our physical appearance and clothing. The non-material and invisible is not more 'holy' than the material and visible. The time when we encounter problems is when our sense of identity comes to rely too much on our physical and outward appearance. 'What we wear and how we look can be a wonderful expression of who we are—but they are not who we are'.[5]

Although our status may have changed, we are still in our mortal bodies, and still need to dress appropriately for the occasion. Being correctly dressed gives us confidence, and that in turn affects our behaviour. If we are secure in that status, if we know we are clothed in garments of salvation, we need not be anxious about our identity. We do not need our clothes to hide behind, to cover up our nothingness, or to project a false image.

> And then what are we left with? What have we got on? Perhaps only what Jesus had on (metaphorically) when he emerged from the tomb, which was the all-covering love of God. He had left his grave clothes behind and was identified only by the love of God which had raised him from the dead, not by any acquisitions, honours or qualifications from his previous life in Galilee.[6]

We can rejoice that our identity is not found in the labels we wear, but rather in relationship with the Father who loves us, and his Son whose death clothes us in righteousness. Like a child, we need to hold on to the hem of Jesus' garment, and follow. We don't necessarily need to know where we're going, but rather who we are going with.[7] Each of us reflects the image of God in a way which no one else can. We need to 'wear ourselves well' as a reflection of the glory of the Lord.

> 'Above all, clothe yourselves with love, which binds everything together in perfect harmony'.
>
> Col. 3:14

'Clothed then with faith and the performance of good works, let us set out on this way with the Gospel for our guide that we may deserve to see Him who has called us to His Kingdom'.

(*The Rule of St. Benedict*, Prologue 21)

**Discussion**

1. Is there anything that has particularly struck you in this exploration of the biblical imagery of clothing?
2. Having read this book, might you discard any of your clothing, literally or symbolically? What might that symbolise?
3. Has this study changed your relationship with God or your attitude to clothes as you go forward?

No condemnation now I dread;
Jesus and all in Him in mine!
Alive in Him, my living Head,
And clothed in righteousness divine,
Bold I approach the eternal throne,
And claim the crown, through Christ my own.

*And can it be*, Charles Wesley (1707–1788)

# PRAYERS

We worship you, O Christ, because for our sake
  you laid aside your power and glory
And clothed yourself in the garment of our humanity,
  to live in poverty here on earth
  and to suffer death upon the cross.
Teach us the lesson of your humility,
  and empty our lives of all pride and selfishness,
That we may find our joy and fulfilment
  in serving others in your name and for your sake.
(Frank Colqohoun, *Contemporary Parish Prayers No. 85)*

*A way to pray Ephesians 6, The Armour of God*

Father God,

I put on the belt of truth around my waist.
Help me to listen to and act upon your truth alone,
Protect me from lies and deception.

I put on the breastplate of righteousness.
Thank you that because of the cross I can be righteous
  in your sight.
Protect my heart from the temptations that come my way.

Help me to live my life in a way that honours you.

I put on the shoes of the gospel of peace.
Then I am ready to take your light wherever you send
   me today.
Help me to walk in the peace and freedom of your Spirit
today, and to leave 'footprints of peace' wherever I go.

I stand behind the shield of faith.
I believe in your power to protect me.
I choose to trust in you, secure in the knowledge of your
   goodness and love.

I place the helmet of salvation on my head.
Jesus you are my salvation.
Thank you that all the riches of heaven are mine
   through you.
Cover my mind and my thoughts, and guard them
   from evil.

I take up the sword of the Spirit.
Holy Spirit, fill me so that I can stand for you today.
Your word is like a two-edged sword.

Help me to hear your voice bringing a word of Scripture
   at my moment of need.
Help me to pray in the Spirit at all times, and to put on
   your armour every day.

You give me all that I need to stand firm in this world.
I ask for your loving and encircling protection, on me
   and around me, now and always.

In Jesus' name,
Amen.

# NOTES

## Introduction

1. The practice of 'dressing' wells in Derbyshire with flowers as a thankfulness for escape from the plague in the 1660s, and continued today.

2. Corrie ten Boom, *The Hiding Place*, p. 204 in 1976 edition.

## 1. Indications of Status

1. See the novel *The Scarlet Letter* by Nathaniel Hawthorne, 1850.

2. http://www.bbc.co.uk/news/magazine-29240820

The power of wearing red 19 Sept 2014; Lisa Jardine

3. See also Gen. 37:34; 2 Kings 19:2; Isa. 37:1–2; Jonah 3:5; Rev. 11:3; black sackcloth made of goat hair, Rev. 6:12.

4. The Cup of Elijah is put on the Passover table in anticipation of his return. When Jesus is on cross, bystanders say he is calling for Elijah who may come to save him (Matt. 27:47, 49).

5. Luke 1; Matt. 3:2; 4:17; 11:9; 14:5; 21:11, 26, 46; 14:1–12; 26–27.

6. In Umberto Eco's novel, *The Name of the Rose*, set in C14, the monks vigorously debated as to whether, and in what way, Christ owned his clothes; this was in relation to their own vows

of poverty.

7. See Num. 15:38–9; Deut. 22:12. Scholars have suggested that when Matthew criticises the scribes and Pharisees for making 'their phylacteries broad and their fringes long' that this may be a reference to enlarging the borders of a prayer shawl, thus making the entire garment larger; see Mark 12:38, referring the scribes 'who like to walk around in long robes'.

8. So also Peter's shadow; Acts 5:15. Early Christian relics (*brandea*) were often ordinary objects which had become holy by coming into contact with holy people or places.

9. *Melote* referring to a sheepskin cloak; *himation* referring to garments in general. In Zech. 13:4 it seems that a 'hairy mantle' was being used as a deception. See also Gen. 25:25.

10. We can see something similar in the record of Aaron passing on his vestments to his son Eleazar Num. 20:22–29.

11. Note here the distinctive waistcoat of Gareth Southgate, Manager of the England football team.

12. This is taken up later with the chief priests, scribes and elders who question Jesus in the temple about his authority. They decide they are unable to answer Jesus' question about John's baptism. Luke 20:1–8; Matt. 21:23–27.

13. See Gen. 41:42 re Joseph.

14. See Baruch's themes of sin, exile, repentance and return (5:1, 2).

15. Paul also argues that this stripping off of the old life, the old self, is comparable, in a way, to circumcision. Circumcision was a symbolic 'divestiture' of a small part of the body; baptism involved a divestiture or stripping off of the entire self; see Col. 2:11f.

16. See *Didache* 7 for variety of practice; ie immersing, sprinkling, pouring; always done in the name of the Father, the Son, and the Holy Spirit.

17. Oxford Dictionary of the Christian Church; entry under Chrysom. This use disappeared in 1552.

18. This may refer to a literal baptism, or Paul may be using 'baptism' here as a metaphor for conversion and identification with Christ. See Dunn, *Galatians*, p. 203.

## 2. Behaving Well

1. *Confessions* VIII.X11

2. Also: Is. 52:1; 2 Chron. 6:41; Job 29:14; 40:10; Ps. 132:9, 16; Zech. 3:1–5

3. Homer, *The Iliad*, 20, 381; see also 9, 231; 19, 36

(Homer, The *Iliad* with an English Translation by A.T. Murray, Ph.D. in two volumes. Cambridge, MA., Harvard University Press; London, William Heinemann, Ltd. 1924.)

4. N.T. Wright, *Paul and the Faithfulness of God* , p. 553

5. Paula Gooder, *Body,* p. 63.

6. So Thompson, *Clothed with Christ*, p. 154.

7. I am grateful to Stephen Barton for some of the following points.

8. RSV translation; NRSV has 'live' rather than 'walk'.

9. See Stephen Barton, *Joy in the NT.*

10. Tom Wright, *Virtue Reborn,* p. 127.

## 3. Being Naked Before God

1. Naked and publicly exposed to shame: Matt. 25:43; 27:35; cf Ps. 22:18; Is. 20:4; see also Col. 2:15: [God] stripped all the spiritual tyrants in the universe of their sham authority at the Cross and marched them naked through the streets (Peterson, *The Message*).

2. A version of the Geneva Bible, printed in 1579, was called the *Breeches Bible,* because the word breeches is used in Gen. 3:7

for the garments made by Adam and Eve.

3. John Goldingay, *Genesis for Everyone*, p. 49.

4. See the warnings against disobedience at the end of Deuteronomy (28:48); see also 2 Chron. 28:15.

5. See also 1 Sam. 19:18–24; Ezek. 23:29.

6. Also Ezek. 18:16. Matt. 25:38, 43, 44; see also Tabitha/Dorcas in Acts 9:36, 39.

7. Note: Is. 6:2, where 'feet' is usually taken to refer to genitals (also Ex. 4:25; Jud. 3:24; 1 Sam. 24:3). Ruth uncovered the 'feet' of Boaz; it is unclear whether this refers to sexual relations since Boaz describes Ruth as a 'woman of noble character' (Ruth 3:11).

8. Gen. 9:20–24: Ham 'saw the nakedness of his father'; when Noah awoke, he knew what his youngest son 'had done to him'; it is possible to interpret this in a sexual way.

9. See also Is. 47:3; Hab. 2:15; Mic. 1:11; Nah. 3:5; Ezek. 23:29.

10. C.S. Lewis, *Voyage of the Dawntreader*, p. 81.

11. Rowan Williams, *Lion's World*, p. 86.

12. Rowan Williams, *Lion's World*, p. 83: 'you will not be able to bring out a 'real self' beneath all the outer layers'. So also Gooder, *Body*, p. 96.

13. Review *Church Times*, 27:01:2012, p. 25; Ruth Burrows, *Love Unknown*, London, Continuum, 2011.

14. Jean Vanier, *Becoming Human*.

15. Henri Nouwen, *In the Name of Jesus,* p. 16.

16. See Vanstone, *Stature of Waiting*.

17. C.S Lewis, *The Great Divorce,* ch. 3 and 12. Williams, *Lion's World*, p. 82, also notes Lewis' general lack of interest in himself: 'He was notoriously uninterested in what he wore and evidently put on the same donnish uniform of shapeless jacket and baggy trousers every morning'.

18. See Rom 8:35: nothing—hardship, distress, persecution, famine, *nakedness*, peril, sword.

## 4. Kinship and Belonging

1. Pliny, *HN* 18:36.

2. Seneca, *On Mercy*, 1:23:2–24:1.

3. As in John Boyne, *The boy in the striped pyjamas,* London, Doubleday 2006; or the orange jumpsuits worn by inmates at Guantanamo Bay. See also 2 Kings 25:29.

4. Rumer Godden, *In this House of Brede*, p. 371.

5. *Church Times,* 27 Sept 2013.

6. George Woodcock, *The British in the Far East;* quoted in Roger Steer, *J. Hudson Taylor,* p. 98.

7. Roger Steer, *J. Hudson Taylor,* p. 176.

8. Merle and Phyllis Good, *20 most asked questions*, p. 23.

9. Marlene Epp; *Mennonite Women in Canada*, p. 183 .

10. Epp, p. 189.

11. As in Aesop's fable of the wolf in sheep's clothing; see also Matt. 10:16; 23:27–28.

12. See also Matt. 7:21–23; 25:31–46.

13. Saracino, *Clothing*, p. 9.

## 5. Christian Clothing?

1. *The Times* article: 3 May 2014.

2. http://www.bbc.co.uk/news/world-us-canada-13320785; accessed 23:07:17. See also debate in the UK, summer 2018, about 'upskirting'.

3. Reference to the twins Agnes Lewis and Margaret Gibson, in Janet Soskice, *The Sisters of Sinai,* p. 254.

4. Michelle Saracino, *Clothing*, p. 38.

5. It is customary to bury a Jewish man in his *tallit* with the

*tzitzit* removed or torn, symbolizing that the deceased can no longer observe the Law.

6. Although in some areas, a minister may feel that wearing robes actually creates less of a barrier than, for instance, wearing a suit.

7. Richard Foster, *Celebration of Discipline*, p. 79.

8. *Epistle to Diognetus*, 5:4

9. Tertullian, *De cultu Feminarum*, (on Female Fashion): Book II, Ch.1, Introduction. Modesty to be observed not only in its essence, but in its accessories.

10. Book II, Ch.5, Some Refinements in dress and personal appearance lawful, some unlawful. Pigments come under the latter head.

11. Book II, Ch.8, Men not excluded from these remarks on personal adornment.

12. Quoted in Marcus Nodder, *City Lives*, p. 168.

13. These verses, along with Eph. 5:22, have given rise to extensive debate on the topic of relationships, especially the phrase, 'wives be submissive to your husbands'. The particular context here in 1 Peter is not necessarily concerned with the subject of women being submissive to men in general, or wives to husbands within marriage, but here the setting is that of a Christian wife married to an unbelieving husband.

14. Henry Fielding, *Tom Jones*, ch. viii.

15. Israel was sustained and guided in the desert by God, who is reliable and generous. This care is represented symbolically by clothes that did not wear out and sandals that did not fall apart (Deut. 8:4; 29:5; Neh. 9:21).

16. 'Look at the flowers—even the Beckhams aren't dressed up like these'; Brian Draper, LICC, Connecting with Culture, 17 October 2014.

17. Michele Saracino, *Clothing*, p. 98.

18. Paula Gooder, *Body*, p. 93.

19. Tom Wright, *Paul for Everyone, 2 Corinthians*, p. 51.

20. John Pritchard, *Living Faithfully*, p. 164.

21. Eugene Petersen, *Jesus Way*, p. 232.

22. N.T. Wright, *Paul*, p. 390.

## 6. The Passion Narratives

1. Mark 8:22–10:52, the central section which also begins with a blind healing, in two stages.

2. This is a Marcan phrase, also at 8:27; 9:33 and 10:17, 32; the way to Jerusalem and the way of suffering, and 'following' used symbolically of discipleship as a journey (1:16–20).

3. Hebrews 12:1 interprets the garment as everything that hinders us, including sin, from running the race set before us.

4. In Mark this is not so much a 'triumphal entry'; the riding takes place outside the city; (11:11). In Mark, this is the only time Jesus enters Jerusalem.

5. RSV translation. NRSV has, 'got up from the table, took off his outer robe', which makes it harder to see the connection with John 10.

6. The word is *tithenai*. Note a progression and development of the concept in John 10:11, 15, 17, 18.

7. The witnesses laid down their garments at the feet of a young man named Saul, at the stoning of Stephen, Acts 7:58.

8. Others have seen a resonance with Amos 2:16:

> 'and those who are stout of heart among the mighty
> Shall flee away naked on that day, says the Lord'.

9. The definition of blasphemy was not at all clear, and later, written Jewish law indicates that the person is only guilty of blasphemy when he clearly pronounces the name of God (*M.Sanh*

7:5). According to this narrow definition, Jesus clearly did not blaspheme against God, because he substituted the word 'Power' for the holy name.

10. See also Gen. 34:29; Lev. 10:6; Josh. 7:6; 2 Sam. 3:31; 13:18–19, 31; 2 K 18:37—19:1; Job 1:20; Ezra 9:3; Acts 2:12; 14:14. The Emperor Augustus tore apparel on hearing of the defeat of Varus in Germany; Cassius Dio in *Roman History* 56:23:1.

11. It is unclear whether in fact the high priest was wearing his official robes, as they may have been locked away by the Romans: see Josephus, *Ant.* 15:11:14.

12. There is also a contrast between 'false testimony' in 26:59, and 'it is not lawful' in 27:6.

13. The links with Jesus' baptism are made more explicit in Mark where the same word is used for 'tearing' (*schizo*, Mark 1:10; 15:38), which also emphasises that both actions are done by God.

14. *Paradidomi*: John 19:16; also 18:30, 36; 19:11. Jesus also 'hands over' his spirit in 19:30.

15. The closest parallel is the mocking of one Karabas in Philo (*In. Flac. 6:36–40*). Some commentators have suggested that John 19:13–16 may extend this scene of mockery if Pilate made Jesus sit on the judgement seat; see also *Gospel of Peter* 3:6–9; Justin, *I Apol.* 35.

16. John 19:24, 28, 36, 37.

17. The opening verse of this psalm is well known: 'My God, my God, why have you forsaken me?' and is recorded by Matthew and Mark as words spoken by Jesus on the cross (27:46; 15:34). They are not recorded by Luke and John. John's passion narrative, in particular, does not record Jesus' anguish here, but focuses on the offering up of his life and his return to the Father.

18. Magonet, *Psalms,* p. 101.

19. Magonet, *Psalms,* p. 102.

20. Josephus *Ant.* III, 161.

21. Would, perhaps, Jesus' clothes and his body still have smelt of the perfume with which he was anointed? Expensive perfume lingers for a long time. I owe this point to David Jenkins.

22. Mark 15:43; Matt. 27:57; Luke 23:50; John 19:38.

23. Tom Wright, *John for Everyone*, p. 141.

24. See Alison Watt's huge painting of draped cloth, *Still*; Old St Paul's Church, Edinburgh, 2004.

25. See *Church Times* 22 Jan 2016, and reference there to C.F.D. Moule's question, 'Where did our Lord get the clothes to wear?' in *Christ Alive and at Large*, Morgan and Moule, Canterbury Press, Norwich, 2011.

26. Matt. 28:3: His appearance was like lightening and his clothing white as snow

Mark 16:5: a young man dressed in a white robe

Luke 24:4: two men in dazzling clothes

John 20:12: two angels in white.

27. Some scholars have seen the transfiguration as a displaced resurrection story, but this lack of mention of Jesus' clothes in the resurrection appearances may suggest otherwise.

28. At that time, to offer a greeting was a religious act and could not be performed without clothing. Thus greetings were not given in the bath, where all were naked (*Y.Berakoth* 2, 4c, 38).

## 7. Conclusion

1. The Hebrew word is unclear here; 'coat of many colours' is the translation in the LXX that found its way into the KJV.

2. The eschatological age was understood to be a time of rest: 4 Ezra 7:36, 38; 8:52; like a great Sabbath: Is. 66:23; Heb. 4:9; as well as a return to a garden: Rev. 22:2; see also Ex. 33:14; Matt. 11:28.

3. See Hooker, *Not Ashamed of the Gospel*, p. 34.

4. 2 Cor. 5:21 sin/righteousness; Gal. 3:13 curse/blessing; 1 Thess. 5:10 death/life; Gal. 4:4f. under the law/free from the law; 2 Cor. 8:9 poor/rich. In 1 Cor. 4:8–13 Paul seems to be arguing that the Corinthians have not accepted the reality of Christ's death and that it has a significance for their lifestyle. He and the other apostles are, amongst other things, foolish, weak, disgraced, hungry, thirsty, clothed in rags, reviled, persecuted and slandered. See also the symbolic change from 'filthy clothes' to 'festal apparel' in Zech. 3:4.

5. Rt Rev Rachel Treweek, *Church Times*, 5 May 2017.

6. John Pritchard, *Living Easter*, p. 55.

7. I owe this point to Rev. Glyn Jones, Chester.

# BIBLIOGRAPHY

Adam, David, *Occasions for Alleluia*, London, SPCK, 2012.

Barton, Stephen, *Joy in the New Testament*, Cambridge, Grove Books, 2013.

Barton, Stephen, *Life Together*, Edinburgh, T&T Clark, 2001.

Boom, Corrie ten, and John and Elizabeth Sherrill, *The Hiding Place,* London, Hodder and Stoughton, Alresford, Christian Literature Crusade, 1972.

Burrows, Ruth, *Love Unknown*, London, Continuum, 2011.

Colquhoun, Frank, (Ed.) *Contemporary Parish Prayers,* London, Hodder and Stoughton, 1975.

Dunn, James, D.G., *The Epistle to the Galatians*, London, A&C Black, 1993.

Epp, Marlene, *Mennonite Women in Canada: A History*, Winnipeg, University of Manitoba Press, 2008.

Fielding, Henry, *The History of Tom Jones, A Foundling,* (1749); here Penguin Classics reprint, Harmondsworth, 2005.

Foster, Richard, *Celebration of Discipline,* London, Hodder and Stoughton, 2008.

Godden, Rumer, *In this House of Brede*, London, Pan Books, 1991, 2nd Edn.

Goldingay, John, *Genesis for Everyone, Part 1*, London, SPCK, 2010.

Good, Merle and Phyllis, *20 Most asked questions about the Amish and Mennonites,* Lancaster PA, Good Books, 1979.

Gooder, Paula, *Body, Biblical spirituality for the whole person,* London, SPCK, 2016.

Hooker, Morna D., *Not Ashamed of the Gospel: New Testament Interpretations of the death of Christ,* Carlisle, Paternoster Press, 1994.

Lewis, C.S., *The Great Divorce,* London, Geoffrey Bles, 1946; and Collins (Fontana Books) 1972.

Lewis, C.S., *The Voyage of the Dawntreader,* London, Geoffrey Bless, 1952; and Collins (Fontana Books) 1980.

Magonet, Jonathan, *A Rabbi Reads the Psalms,* London, SCM Press, 1994 and 2004.

Nodder, Marcus, *City Lives,* Leyland, 10 Of Those, 2018.

Nouwen, Henri, *In the Name of Jesus,* London, Darton, Longman & Todd, 1989.

Peterson, Eugene H., *The Jesus Way: A Conversation on the Ways that Jesus is the Way,* Cambridge, Eerdmans, 2007.

Peterson, Eugene H., *The Message,* Colorado Springs, NavPress, 1993.

John Pritchard, *Living Easter through the Year, Making the most of the resurrection,* London, SPCK, 2005.

Pritchard, John, *Living Faithfully,* London, SPCK, 2013.

Pritchard, John, *Going to Church: A User's Guide,* London, SPCK, 2009.

Radcliffe, Timothy, *Take the Plunge, Living Baptism and Confirmation,* London, Bloomsbury, 2012.

Saracino, Michele, *Clothing,* Minneapolis, Fortress Press, 2012.

Soskice, Janet, *The Sisters of Sinai*, New York, Alfred A Knopf, 2009.

Steer, Roger, *J. Hudson Taylor, A Man in Christ*, Milton Keynes, OMF/Authentic Media, 2001.

Thompson, Michael B., *Clothed with Christ: The Example and Teaching of Jesus in Romans 12:1–15:13*, Sheffield, JSNTS, Sheffield Academic Press, 1991.

Vanier, Jean, *Becoming Human*, New Jersey, Paulist Press, 1998.

Vanstone, W.H., *Stature of Waiting*, London, Darton, Longman and Todd, 1982.

Ward, Simon, *The Character of Fashion*, London, White Bench, 2016.

Watson, Andrew, *The Way of the Desert*, Abingdon, The Bible Reading Fellowship, 2011.

Williams, Rowan, *The Lion's World: A journey into the heart of Narnia*, London, SPCK, 2012.

Wright, N.T., *Paul and the Faithfulness of God*, London, SPCK, 2013.

Wright, Tom, *John for Everyone, Part 2*, London, SPCK, 2002.

Wright, Tom, *Paul for Everyone, 2 Corinthians*, London, SPCK, 2003.

Wright, Tom, *Virtue Reborn*, London, SPCK, 2010.

# INDEX OF BIBLICAL REFERENCES

# ABOUT THE AUTHOR

Frances taught for over 20 years the Gospels module of the Guildford Diocesan Ministry Course, as well as being a Tutor for degree level courses on Matthew and Mark's Gospels. During this time she completed a PhD and this was published as *Discernment of Revelation in the Gospel of Matthew*, by Peter Lang, in their Religions and Discourse Series.

She has also written study notes for Churches Together in Godalming, for use in their ecumenical Lent study groups: a) *Mark's Gospel; b) The Seven Last Words of Jesus; c) The Beatitudes; d) Building God's House, Studies in John's Gospel*; as well as personal meditation material on the theme of *Footsteps* at the request of and published by the Fellowship of Prayer for Unity.

She is married to Peter, and gave up paid employment as a religious books editor when their first child was born. She is passionate about literacy and theological education, and works as a Director and Company Secretary of Grove Books Ltd, based in Cambridge. She is also a Trustee of Feed the Minds, an ecumenical charity funding functional literacy projects in the developing world, and Chair of the United Society for Christian Literature.

She is an active member of her local Anglican Church in Surrey, England, and is currently serving as Churchwarden for a second period of office. She mentors a number of people in ministry of various kinds, in a spiritual companion role. She has three children and, at present, five grandchildren.